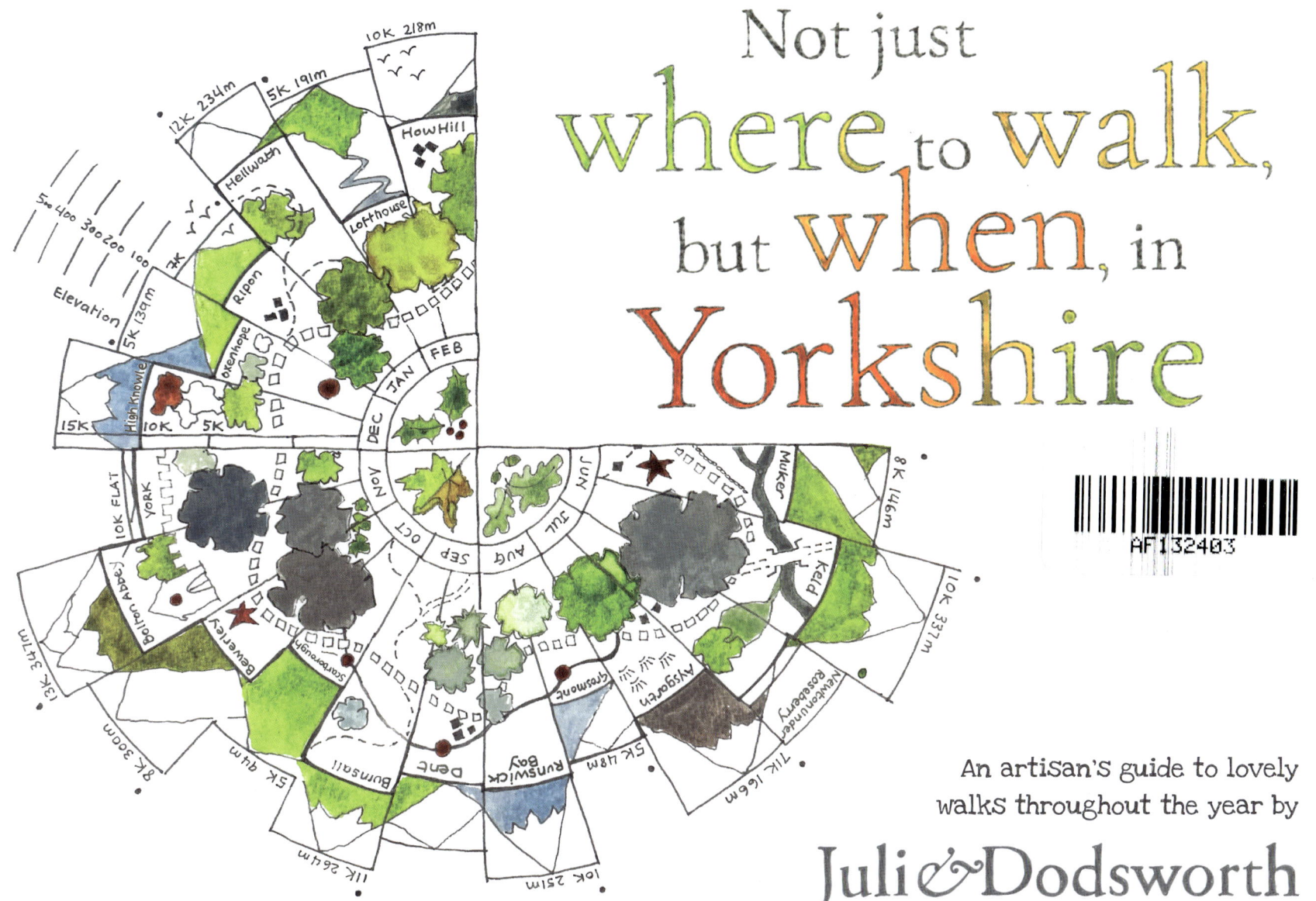

Not just where to walk, but when, in Yorkshire

An artisan's guide to lovely walks throughout the year by

Juli&Dodsworth

First published 2025
© 2025 Julie Dodsworth
Reprinted 2026

All rights reserved. No part of this publication may be reproduced, stored in a retrieval system, or transmitted by any means, electronic, mechanical, photocopying, recording or otherwise, without the prior written permission of the copyright holder and publishers.

COUNTRYSIDE BOOKS
3 Catherine Road
Newbury, Berkshire, RG14 7NA

To view our complete range of books please visit us at
www.countrysidebooks.co.uk

ISBN 978 1 84674 437 2

All materials used in the manufacture of this book carry FSC certification.

Designed and Typeset by Inc-dot Design & Print, York and KT Designs, St Helens
Printed by Holywell Press, Oxford

A dedication
To my Mother & Father
Mary & Dennis Copley

Their desire for & knowledge of a 'lovely walk'
has cascaded down through our family.

Our thanks for such a wonderful gift & legacy.

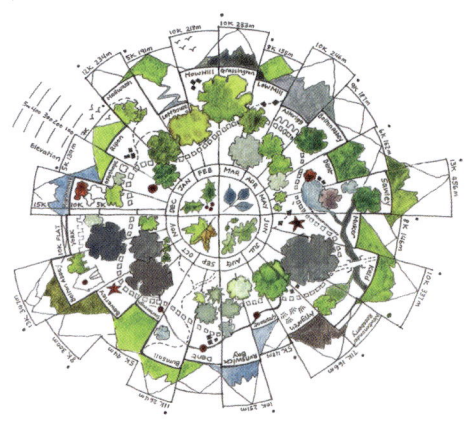

Contents

				Page
	Key			5
	Area Map			6-7
	Introduction			8

The Walks

Month	Walk	Title	Area	Distance	
Jan	1	The Amazing Wetlands of Ripon	Ripon & Littlethorpe	7k / 4½ miles	12
Jan	2	The Medieval Environs of Fountains Abbey	Fountains Abbey	11.5k / 7¼ miles	14
Feb	3	Gorgeous Gorges	Lofthouse & Middlesmoor	4k / 2½ miles	18
Feb	4	The How Hill Mountain	Studley Roger & How Hill	10k / 6 miles	20
Mar	5	The Wobbly Bridge Walk	Grassington, Linton, Thorpe & Hebden	10k / 6 miles	24
Mar	6	Poetry Walk	Low Mill & Farndale	8.5k / 5¼ miles	26
Apr	7	The Waterfalls of Askrigg	Askrigg	5k / 3 miles	30
Apr	8	Bluebell Heaven	Bolton Abbey	8.5k / 5¼ miles	32
May	9	The Wonders of Dentdale	Dent	6k / 3¾ miles	36
May	10	Outstanding Natural Beauty of Eavestone Lake	Sawley & Eavestone	9k / 5½ miles	38
Jun	11	World Heritage Wonders of Swaledale	Muker & Ivelet	8k / 5 miles	42
Jun	12	Up and Over Kisdon Fell	Keld & Muker	8.5k / 5¼ miles	44
Jul	13	Yorkshire Matterhorn	Newton under Roseberry	6.5k / 4 miles	48
Jul	14	The Magic of Aysgarth Falls	Aysgarth & West Burton	7k / 4½ miles	50
Aug	15	Full Steam Ahead on the North York Moors	Goathland, Beck Hole & Grosmont	6k / 3¾ miles	54
Aug	16	Sandcastles and Hobgoblins	Runswick Bay	9k / 5½ miles	56
Sep	17	The Waterfalls of Dent	Dent	8k / 5 miles	60
Sep	18	Secret Passageways	Burnsall, Linton & Hebden	10k / 6 miles	62
Oct	19	A Walk for Small Children	Scarborough	4k / 2½ miles	66
Oct	20	Our Little Lake District	Bewerley	8k / 5 miles	68
Nov	21	Autumn Splendour at Bolton Abbey	Bolton Abbey	13k / 8 miles	72
Nov	22	Firecracker City Walk	York	10k / 6 miles	74
Dec	23	Yorkshire Stonehenge	High Knowle	7.5k / 4¾ miles	78
Dec	24	The Mince Pie Special	Oxenhope, Haworth & Oakworth	5k / 3 miles	80
		Walking Notes			82

Key

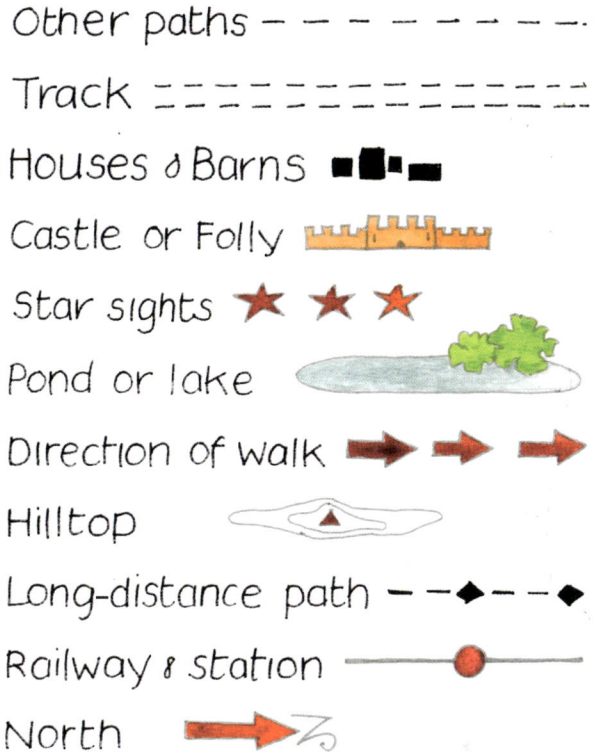

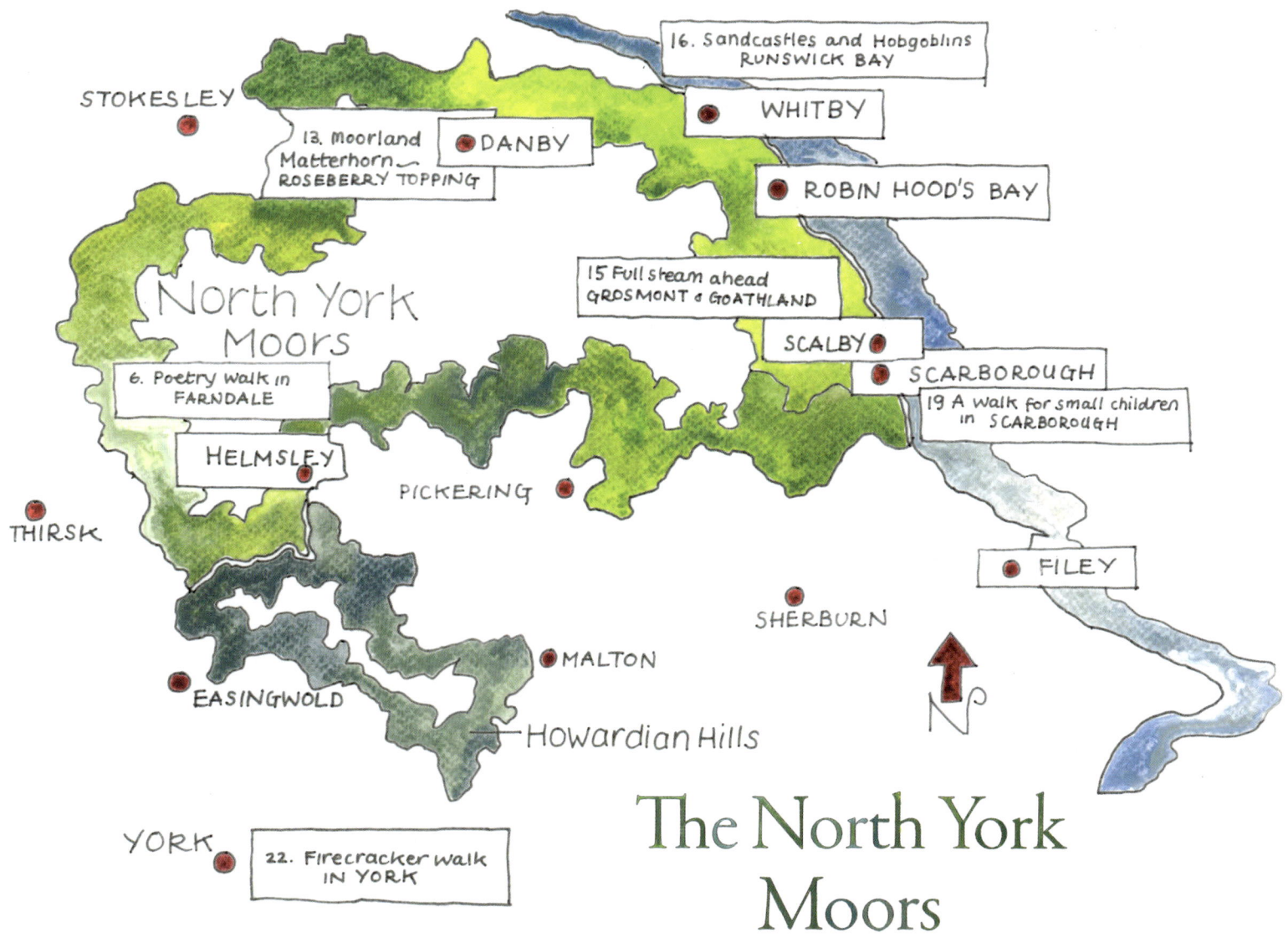

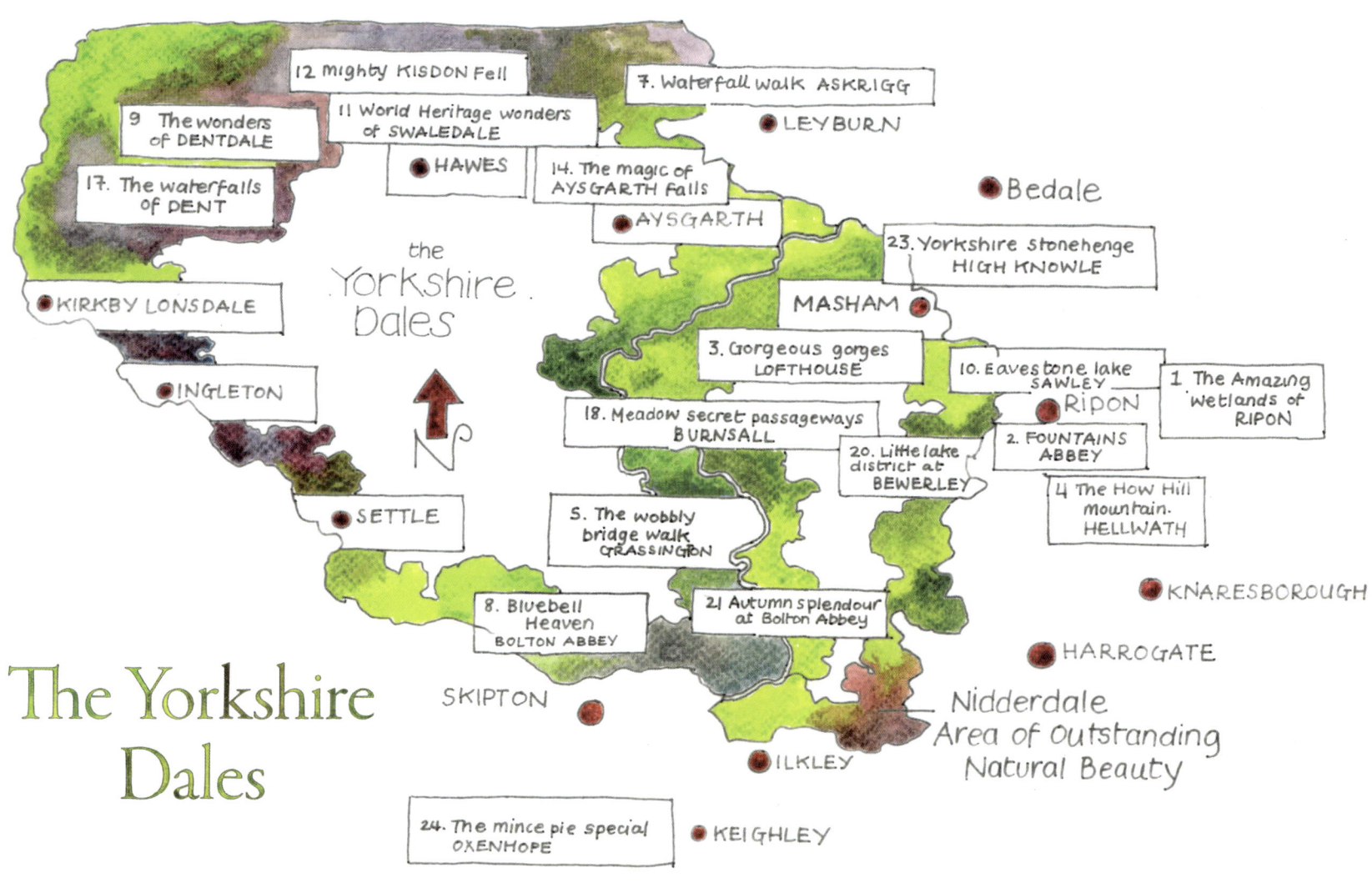

Dear lovely walker,

Welcome to our first collection of walks in Yorkshire, suggestions of where to go and moreover ... when. How did this all happen?

After 30 years of taking walks in our beloved 'God's own country' with our growing family, friends visiting Yorkshire would call and ask me 'what would be a nice walk Julie?'

Oakworth Station.

I was always happy to draw a sketch but would add 'I would go here at this time of year because ... it's easy to park ... it's the right place for the weather ... you wouldn't want to miss ... ... you can only see such and such this week ... and so forth.

So, these are very personal notes. I have loved exploring, catching Mother Nature at her very best, remembering these walks for you and making these sketches.

There are many famous places that have not made it into this collection, only for the reason they are often just too busy and/or are very well documented elsewhere. My favourite walks help us escape the crowds ... or adversely, to use busier times to our advantage.

Of course all of our walks can be lovely at any time of the year. Late Spring when the world bursts into life and that gorgeous golden light of late October are our favourites. But I'm hoping there are some things you, like me, wouldn't want to miss ... the Oxenhope Mince pie special, the Bluebells of the late Spring or the amazing Ripon wetlands winter murmurations to name just a few.

If you are new to walking, I urge you to invest in some 'proper walking attire' ... breathable base layer clothing, a waterproof walking coat, walking boots, waterproof over trousers, sunscreen, rucksack and map are a must. It's worth noting ... now you are a proper walker (!) jeans, wellies and woolly jumpers are very unsuitable for your activity.

Always take some refreshment & energy snacks and practise following your OS map and compass.

Most of all just enjoy! If you ever feel lost (hopefully the sketches and notes work for you!) refer to your OS map and remember other walkers will always be glad to help. Yorkshire is super friendly! Failing that, simply retrace your steps to a place where you know you are safe is great maxim to follow.

St. John's Knaresborough

This is a good place for me to wax lyrical on the virtues of the OS WALKER & BIKER APP. I resisted this for years ... nothing was going to replace the reliability of the paper map ... but by the magic of the wonder web(!) the App tells you exactly where you are, and you can plot and follow your route to be doubly sure exactly where you are. As said, if you are a little new to walking it can be an amazing help to your navigation.

I know you will fall in love with our walks just as we have done over the years and you can enjoy them over and over again within our lovely county. You'll get to know some secret places (remember to keep them secret!) and you will soon be coming up with suggestions of your own!

New hobbies are there to be had ... Photography, birdwatching, local history, fauna, flora and charity walking to name but a few, or simply feeling a little healthier in mind and body is just wonderful.

So let's get our gear together and go for a walk. Some of the best paths in the world are awaiting.

And lastly two thoughts of gratitude. One for the blessing of North Yorkshire where we have seaside, moorland, ancient woodlands, dales, hills and the most wonderful medieval city, all in one glorious county and secondly to you lovely walker for sharing your time with us through the pages of this book.

Wishing you the most wonderful walking days.

Julie

Fountains Abbey

- The Amazing Wetlands of Ripon - Ripon & Littlethorpe
- The Medieval Environs of Fountains Abbey - Fountains Abbey

January is probably one of the most challenging months to find the motivation for us to simply 'go for a walk'. Short days and cold inclement weather all seem to be against us. But, as my Dad would say, 'No such thing as bad weather ... just the wrong clothes!'. And so, I agree. With warm, layered, breathable clothing and your proper walking boots, the Yorkshire countryside is waiting for us.

Keeping to the fringes of the Moors and Dales takes us to less hilly walks and nearer to the main roads - all a little easier at this time of year.

Our January chosen walks are both in the environs of Ripon - simply perfect for a winter walk. Murmurations and medieval majesty await. And the best bit? Whilst the world is hibernating you can have the Yorkshire countryside all to yourself!

Renton Bridge, Ripon Canal

Ripon & Littlethorpe

Distance 7 k / 4½ miles
Allow 2 hrs plus time to watch the murmuration
Ascent 33 m

Start of walk / parking
Canalside House
7 Charter Road
Ripon
HG4 1AJ

 Useful info

http://www.ripononline.co.uk

https://riponcathedral.org.uk

Yorkshire wildlife trust / Ripon Wetlands

https://www.ywt.org.uk/nature-reserves/ripon-city-wetlands

Your best map

OS Map of Ripon & Boroughbridge
Easingwold
299 1:25 000

Our walk starts at the canal-side car park just east of the city centre of Ripon. A 10 minute walk into the city centre is along the canalside path where you would find shops, cafés, pubs and the beautiful medieval Ripon Cathedral.

Our walk is taking us in the opposite direction - around the racecourse, along the river Ure, through the wetlands and back up the canal.

A mainly one-level walk full of interest, wildlife and away from the crowds. The jewel in the crown is to catch the starling murmurations in the winter months.

You will need to time your walk to finish around dusk (about 4 pm) for you to experience the most amazing whirling cacophony as the birds gather before they roost for the night over the wetlands.

Ripon canal and basin are at one of the most northern points on the canal and river network. It offers a fascinating canalside walk to the river confluence where you can stop and view from 'hides' other visiting birds over the wetlands.

All in all a super walk for a January day - wildlife and countryside in abundance without the challenge that hills and winter can bring.

The Amazing Wetlands of Ripon

JANUARY A walk almost all on one level around the environs of the RIPON WETLANDS.

The star of the show - the incredible starling murmurations at dusk. Be prepared to be wowed on our lovely easy walk for all. **NOTE! THE WETLAND PART OF YOUR WALK IS OUT OF BOUNDS TO DOGS.**

A to B

From the car park head towards the racecourse across the car park/field. With the road on your left walk in front of the racecourse until your path brings you to the corner of the road that crosses the river.

B to C

Without crossing the river take the path just at the corner of the bridge and head to the WETLANDS. A clear path for 1k ahead (with the river on your left) takes you to a path on your right which you follow to the canal.

C to D

At the canal turn left and follow the path all the way to the lock. At the lock, cross over and walk back up the canal to the bridge. Take the lane rising to your left all the way to meet a quiet road.

D to finish

At the quiet road turn right and head through LITTLETHORPE. At the pretty church turn right and continue straight ahead onto a lane to cross the canal. Turn left to walk alongside the canal (now on your left) to the car park.

NOTE

To catch the murmuration, time your walk to finish at dusk. It may not happen every year - check social media for sightings over the winter months. You can take your dog by the canal but the wetlands are out of bounds.

Fountains Abbey

Distance 11.5 k / 7¼ miles
Time 4 hrs
Ascent 234 m

Start of walk /park
(alongside the playing fields)
Hell Wath Lane
Ripon
HG4 2JT

Or the National Trust car park
Fountains Abbey and Studley
Royal Water Garden
Studley Park
Ripon
HG4 3DY

i Useful info

A lovely ramble around the environs of the stunning Fountains Abbey. It's always lovely to be able to access a great walk that is near to the main road networks over winter. Thus this walk is an absolute treasure - so much interest along the way without the challenge that the hills and winter can bring.

Be prepared to experience deer, medieval architecture, winding paths, little bridges, weirs, lakes, migrating birds, waterfalls and lovely Italian styled 'views'.

The walk is easy to navigate and can be made shorter (cut across from y to x) if the weather is just too unkind and or time is pressing.

There are cafés, loos & gift shops along the way, all of the very high standards of the National Trust.

To pass through the grounds of the abbey there will be a charge or free to National Trust members. Parking at the optional start and walking through the grounds will both be at a charge or once again free to National Trust members.

https://www.nationaltrust.org.uk/visit/yorkshire/fountains-abbey-and-studley-royal-water-garden

Your best map
OS Map of Ripon & Boroughbridge, Easingwold,
299 1:25 000
And Map of Nidderdale, Fountains Abbey,
Ripon & Pateley Bridge
298 1:25 000 (Fountains Abbey is on the edge of both maps)

Or smaller scale on one OS map of Northallerton & Ripon
Pateley Bridge & Leyburn 99 1:50 000

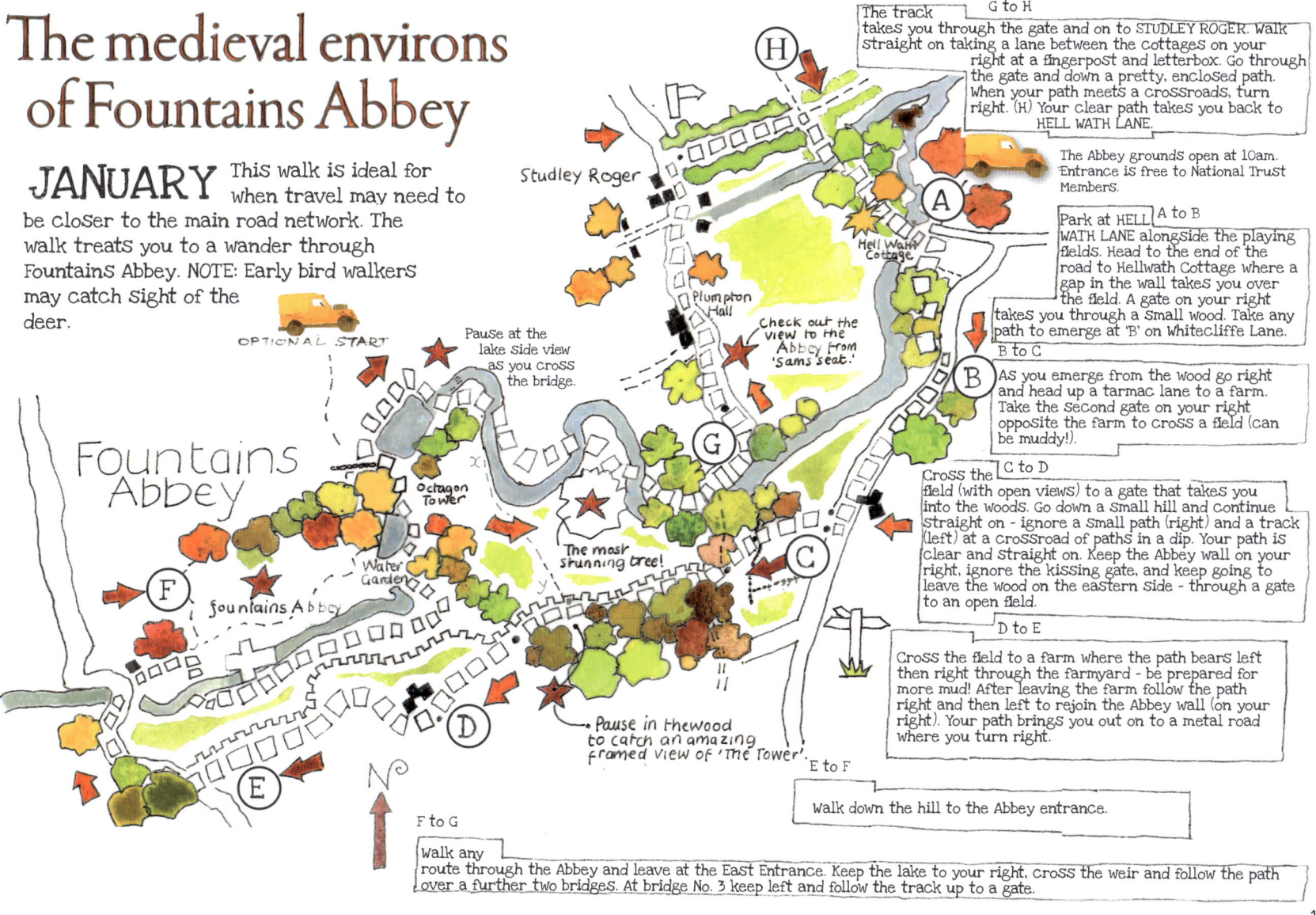

- **Gorgeous Gorges - Lofthouse & Middlesmoor**
- **The How Hill Mountain - Studley Roger & How Hill**

February will soon fly by. My lovely mum would always say 'Spring is just a snowdrop away'.

Parks and city/town walks can help us to blow some cobwebs away. The crocuses on Harrogate Stray just seem to herald that spring is on its way. The riverside walks in York and Ripon are easy to access and can help us to get our walking mojo.

For us, we can take an adventure into the outstandingly beautiful Nidd Gorge from Lofthouse. The Victorians called this their 'little Switzerland' - so much to explore and keep the family interested!

Your journey to Lofthouse weaves up the valley passing Gouthwaite Reservoir. Here is a Site of Special Scientific Interest and a renowned bird sanctuary. It's a great location to spot waders and wildfowl on the water and soaring raptors above the heather.

A lovely hill to climb at How Hill in the environs of Fountains Abbey will complete your step out into early spring. This is your 'water cooler walk'! A chance to really show off your climb and tell of your view over fifty miles from a place very few have heard of.

And so as you sit on How Hill (congratulating yourself) take time to promise yourself many, many returns. Those beautiful oak trees below will soon be in bud, racing against the bluebells at their feet.

A true Yorkshire gem and a stunning day to remember.

Lofthouse & Middlesmoor

Distance 4 k / 2½ miles
Time 1 hr 30 mins
Ascent 191 m

Start of walk /park at the lay-by on the bend near the entrance to Studfold Adventure Trail

Optional parking at Studfold Farm Lofthouse Harrogate HG3 5SG

i Useful info

https://www.howstean.co.uk (Check for open times)

Your best map
OS Map of Nidderdale 298
1:25 000

A gem of a walk at any time of year. We love this excursion in February as there are adventures to be had at How Stean Gorge if a little extra walking is needed in the February half term with children in tow! Most certainly our children loved the cave walk and gorge explorations back in the day (and still do!).

Our walk starts in Lofthouse (pub, shop & facilities) or at Studfold Farm - day parking. A climb up to Middlesmoor is rewarded with a wonderful view of Nidderdale from the most amazing ancient Yorkstone path.

A meadow to meadow walk follows as you drop back down to the river. From here we simply follow the river along a beautiful enchanted gorge. So so pretty!

Here lies our first secret path! Your peace and tranquility of the gorge prequels the honey pot of How Stean and all the attractions it has to offer.

Do revisit in the summer. I remember every picnic we've enjoyed on the banks of the 'secret gorge'. The water so shallow.. the children enjoying a little paddle. Lovely memories of this little Eden in Yorkshire's own area of outstanding beauty.

Gorgeous gorges

February

A lovely walk to earmark for the winter months. If the weather is just too wintry, a trip to the cave at HOW STEAN GORGE★ could be a great add on (if the walk is shortened too). Be sure to keep this walk in the diary for early summer too - when the walk takes you into the most enchanted beck and gorge.

B to C
After a little explore around MIDDLESMOOR, head downhill on the road and turn right into the last farm.

A to B
Park at the lay-by on the bend near the entrance to Studfold Adventure Trail and take the footpath that will take you up the hill. Follow the markers through a farm and continue to the Yorkstone path into MIDDLESMOOR.

C to D to E
From the farm traverse down the hill through slit stiles and gates to a stile leading into the wood. Have a little explore around the footbridge before retracing your steps a little to follow a new path. Here just keep the river on your right all the way to HOW STEAN.

E to F
At the HOW STEAN GORGE visitor centre head left down the road back to LOFTHOUSE.

Take a detour to Low Riggs

Have a little explore around the footbridge

Well House

caves and gorge on a small scale

MIDDLESMOOR

A Yorkstone path a wow view of NIDDERDALE.

Half Way House

HOW STEAN GORGE

LOFTHOUSE

Studfold FARM.

N

4

Studley Roger & How Hill

Distance 10 k / 6 miles
Time 3 to 4 hrs
Ascent 218 m

Start of walk /park
Hell Wath Lane (alongside the playing fields)
Ripon
HG4 2JT

i **Useful info**

OS Map of Ripon & Boroughbridge
Easingwold
299 1:25 000
&
Map of Nidderdale
Fountains Abbey, Ripon & Pateley Bridge
298 1:25 000
(Fountains Abbey is on the edge of both maps)
Or smaller scale on one map.
Map of Northallerton & Ripon
Pateley Bridge & Leyburn. 99 1:50 000

When Spring is just a snowdrop away this lovely walk will have all the adventure of a good hill climb without venturing into the ... hills!

Our walk starts once again at Hellwath (no facilities but there is a very nice coffee wagon Wednesdays to Saturdays on the footie pitch) and takes us for a grand step out all the way up Whitcliffe Lane.

With grand views all the way, your last push is up the permissive path to How Hill Tower. Here you can see for over 50 miles to Roseberry Topping and beyond.

The walk returns through the woods and environs of Fountains Abbey ... downhill all the way. You will certainly blow away some winter cobwebs and have some impressive pictures to take home.

A little more about the Tower:

How Hill Tower is built on the site of the Chapel of Saint Michael de Monte. The hill with the village of Erlesholt (now deserted) was given by Robert de Sartis to Fountains Abbey and the chapel was built in c1200. It was repaired or rebuilt around 1494. This tower was built by John Aislabie. It was part of the first phase of the garden at Studley Park in c1718.

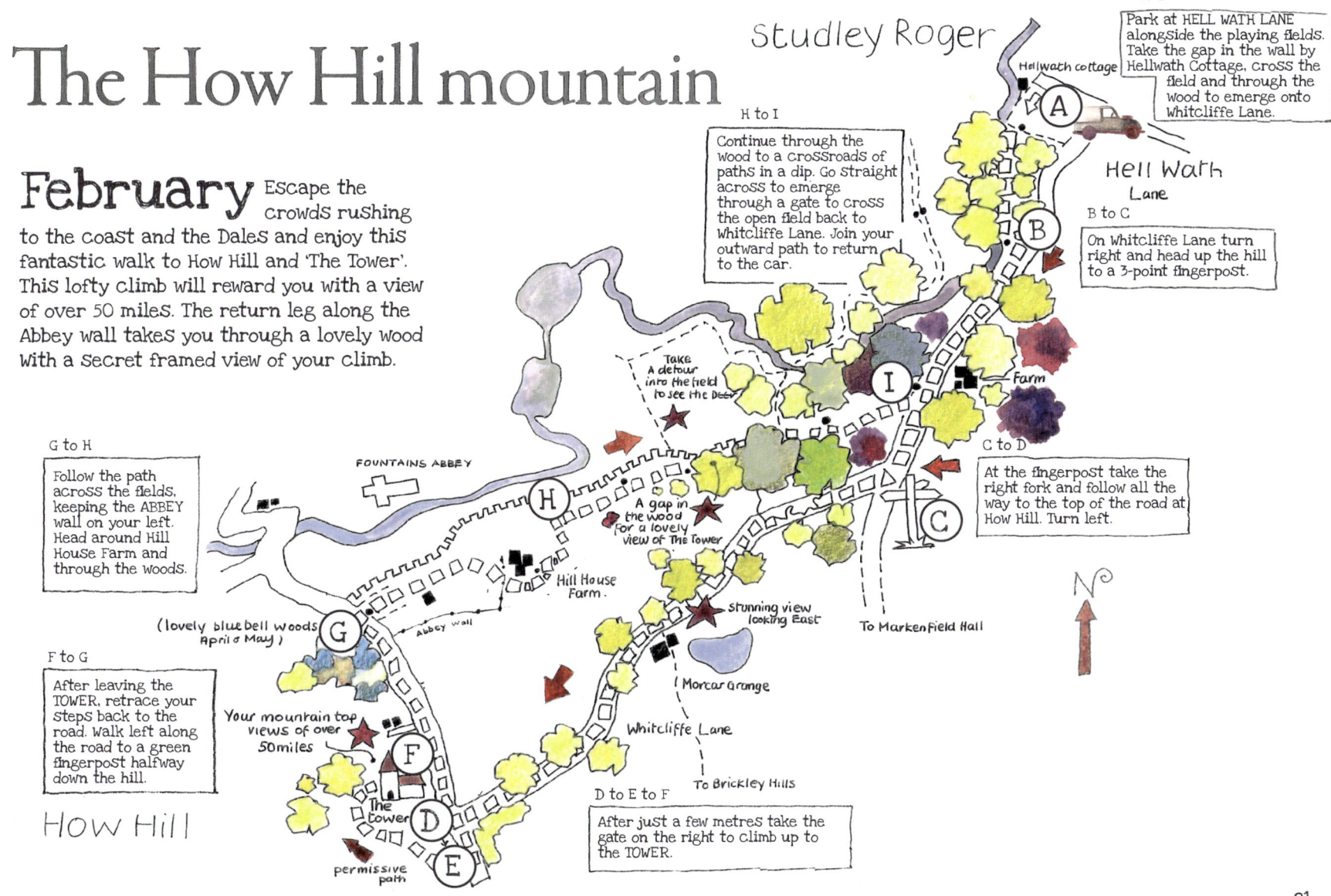

- **The Wobbly Bridge Walk - Grassington, Linton, Thorpe & Hebden**
- **Poetry Walk - Low Mill & Farndale**

The weather men will tell you the 1st of March is the first day of spring. I'm more old-school and patiently wait for the spring equinox around the 21st. Then we really can celebrate! Daylight hours now are longer than the night and the countryside is rushing into bud. With something new to see every day, March is a month to savour.

To head up into the Dales and Moors in March is as much on the calendar as Christmas. Our chosen walks take us to the environs of Hebden and Farndale.

The Dales Way beckons with bobbing yellow primroses and the first of those lovely lambs. Then sings my soul! Our first walk includes what my children always called 'the wobbly bridge' - more officially known as Hebden Suspension Bridge.

The legend is that the bridge was commissioned in 1884, following the drowning of a local man while trying to cross the stepping stones over the River Wharfe.

The new bridge was designed as a suspension bridge and was built by the village blacksmith, William Bell. A grand opening was held in 1885 with a brass band and a picnic tea. For us, it is a chance to feel that sway and wobble as we cross. A great place for us to take our picnic too, toast all those who cross and to savour the moment - beautiful, amazing, springtime is here.

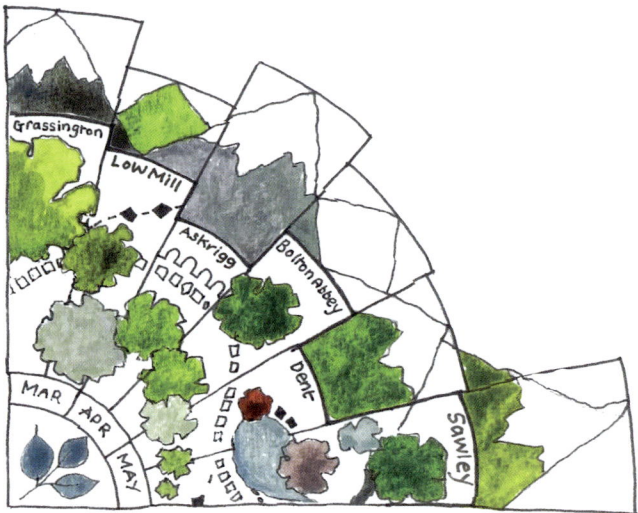

Grassington, Linton, Thorpe & Hebden

Distance 10 k / 6 miles
Time 3 hrs
Ascent 233 m

Start of walk /park
Grassington National Park Centre
Hebden Road
Grassington
BD23 5LB

i Useful info

www.yorkshiredales.org.uk/places/grassington_national_park_centre/

Map of Yorkshire Dales - Southern & Western Areas
OL2 1:25 000

A lovely walk around the environs of Grassington, Linton and Hebden in the heart of the Yorkshire Dales.

Our walk has some lovely star features - the waterfalls, a very pretty church and the very wobbly suspension bridge at Hebden!

Grassington is a day trip destination in its own right. Lots of pubs, cafés and many different shops. There are facilities where you park at the National Park visitor centre and the car park itself has lots of overflow for busier times.

Grassington always seems to come calling around mid March. Your journey there will see the flush of green on the hedgerows and all those other lovely first signs of Spring. Creamy yellow primroses and lambs in the fields complete our picture of Spring heaven.

Last of all ... is first of all ... our walk starts at a gorgeous paved enclosed path down to the falls ... and I wonder ... who has walked this path before us over the hundreds of years? Quite a thought isn't it?

The wobbly bridge walk

March A ride up into the Yorkshire Dales in the early spring will always shake off those winter blues. You'll see the first lambs and a flush of green on the hedgerows. A mainly low-level walk with lots of interest all the way.

A to B
From the car park take the enclosed path down to the falls. Turn immediately right after the bridge and follow the path keeping the RIVER WHARFE on your right. Emerge on the road, turn left and walk on to the school.

B to C
From the school, take the gate to walk over the field to the next road.

C to D
Cross the road to take a path over an open field, a beck and under an old railway bridge to LINTON.

D to E
In LINTON, keep the village green on your right and cross the river by a small bridge. After the bridge turn right up the lane, past the cottages to a farm. Take the path signposted around the farm and keep dead ahead up the hill (ignoring other paths left and right). Keep going all the way up the hill until you meet a stile leading onto Thorpe Lane.

E to F
Turn left onto the lane passing a lovely enclosed path on your left. Keep on the lane through THORPE all the way down to a T-junction. (Ignore a track on your right to Burnsall.)

F to G
At the T-junction, cross the road and take a footpath ahead to descend down the steep hill to cross the WHARFE by the bridge (or stepping stones!). Turn immediately left to take the Dales Way back to GRASSINGTON.

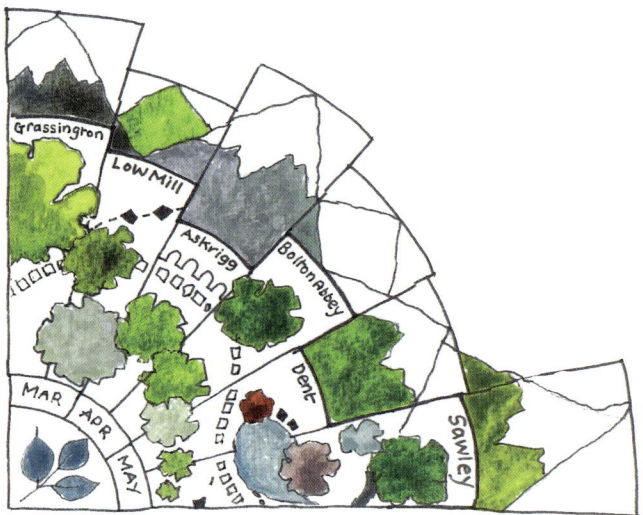

Low Mill & Farndale

Distance 8.5 k / 5¼ miles
Time 3 hrs
Ascent 155 m

Start of walk /park
Low Mill Car Park
Farndale
North York Moors
YO62 7UY

i **Useful info**

Your best map
OS Explorer OL26 North York Moors, Western Area

A not so secret very easy riverside walk of the famous Daffodils of Farndale. The flowers are at their best in late March but it may be super busy ... So, I would recommend to try to avoid the weekends.

Low Mill has a generous sized (pay and display) car park, loos and a shop that serves hot drinks alongside other fare.

The path to Church House (and pub!) is incredibly easy to follow and you can enjoy those bobbing daffodils along the way! At Church House I've added an extra ramble... an alternative return route (to simply retracing your steps) which is more undulating, has quite a few ladder stiles and lots of mud!

There are yellow markers and fingerposts at most gates but the price of your welcome peace from the crowds is that the field-to-field paths are little walked and therefore somewhat sketchy. Your OS App with the trusty red arrow or map & compass may be needed.

Saying all that, this really is a little gem of a walk in a beautiful setting. The walk by the river Dove, the little villages and St Mary's church are not to be missed.

Poetry walk

C to D to E
Turn right at North Gill onto the lane to the road. Turn right to pick up a signpost down to the church. Leave the church onto the road, turn left and a short climb to pick up a path on your right.

E to F to G
Once on your path take a clearly signed path on your left after only a few metres. Keep ahead through Bragg Farm - keep right to Bitchagreen.

G to finish
Keep ahead to High Wold and then follow yellow signs to LOW MILL.

A to B
From the car park follow the path clearly marked 'Public Path to High Mill' to the daffodils. You will pass the Daffy Caffy and finish at CHURCH HOUSES.

B to C
From CHURCH HOUSES take the 2nd left road to Hall Farm. Walk through the farm and up over the hill - through Head House (past the old Series II Land Rover on your left) down the hill over the footbridge, through the bog - up to North Gill.

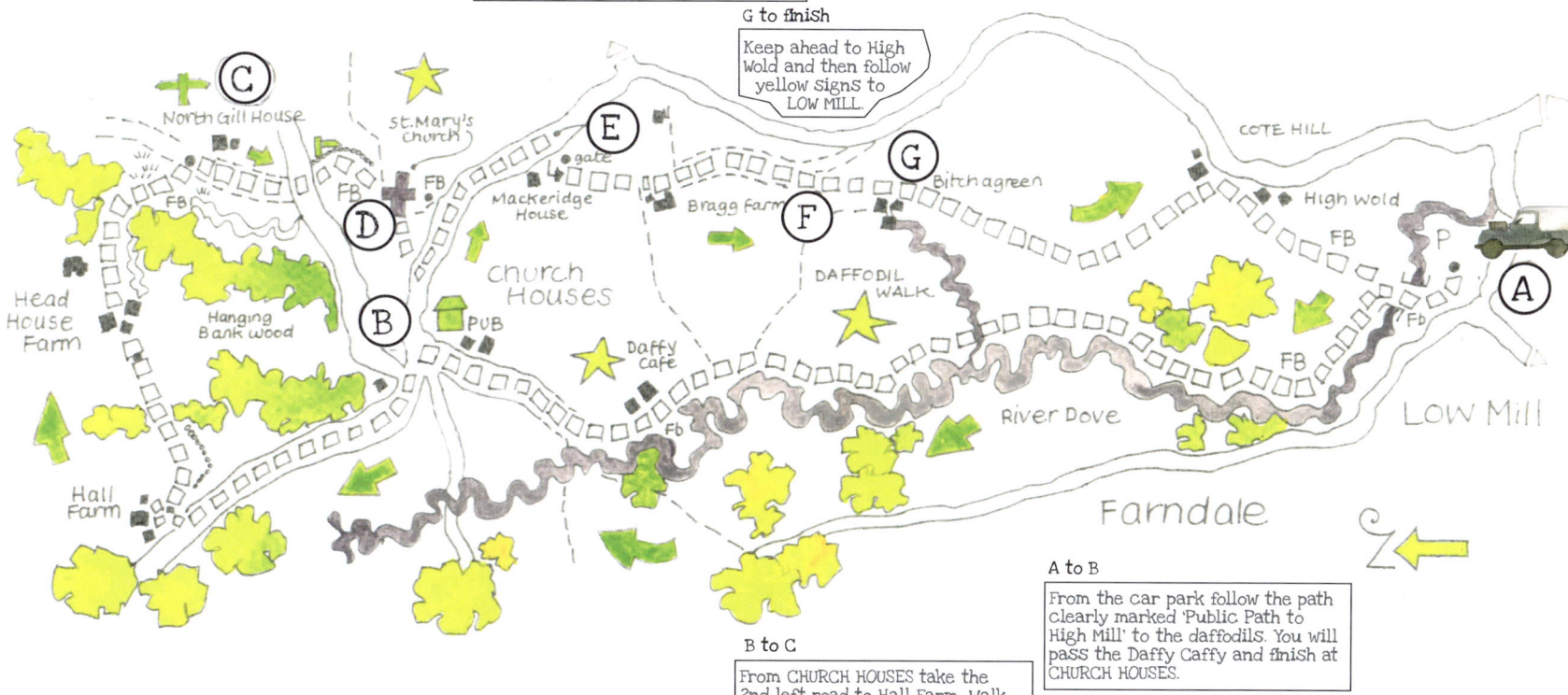

March
A gentle stroll along the River Dove to experience the famous poetry-inspiring daffodils. A lovely farm to farm ramble to follow to help escape the crowds.

- The Waterfalls of Askrigg - Askrigg
- Bluebell Heaven - Bolton Abbey

April. What can I say? For me, this is the most dynamic and beautiful month, full of firsts with every day something new to see. I always feel that springtime in April comes rushing in and I almost want to hold my hands up and say 'whoa! slow down!'

For us, the Yorkshire countryside awaits and I would say any walk in our book will be a wonder to you. There truly is nothing to compare with the paths and lanes of North Yorkshire. Well signposted, up and down dale, through farmyards, woodlands and meadows where we feel welcome and trusted to enjoy some of the best walking to be had anywhere in the world.

And so from the countryside flora and fauna banquet on offer I've chosen to take you to the environs of Bolton Abbey and Askrigg. The bluebells on the Devonshire estate (in flower throughout most of April) are a haze of beauty. Every year we return to pay homage to the finest, most stunning, completely gorgeous, floral display.

River Wharfe, Bolton Abbey

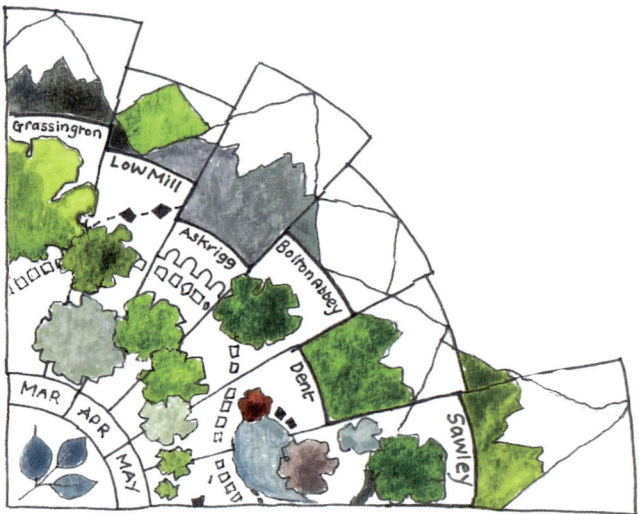

Askrigg

Distance 5 k / 3 miles
Time 2 to 3 hrs
Ascent 237 m

Start of walk /park
Askrigg village car park
Leyburn Road
Askrigg
DL8 3HD

i Useful info

Your best map
OS Explorer Yorkshire Dales Northern & Central areas
OL 30 1:25 000

OL26 North York Moors Western area

O ur lovely walk starts in the pretty, iconic village of Askrigg. There is a small village car park, two pubs, cafés, a plant nursery and artisan shops. Modest facilities are by the village Hall.

Our first star of the show is Mill Dam - a gorgeous Yorkstone path across the flower meadow, an aqueduct and waterfall!

Our walk takes us almost immediately into beautifully wooded Mill Gill - climbing all the way to Whitfield Gill Force.

The last 400 m clamber over large boulders and fallen tree trunks to the force is quite an adventure .. but you will be wowed!

A lovely step out on the return journey rewards us with views of grandeur.

This is the perfect walk when we have time for a 'day in the Dales'. The clambering and sense of exploration makes this a great walk for getting the teenagers off the Easter holidays sofa - lots to see in an action packed fairly short and do-able walk!

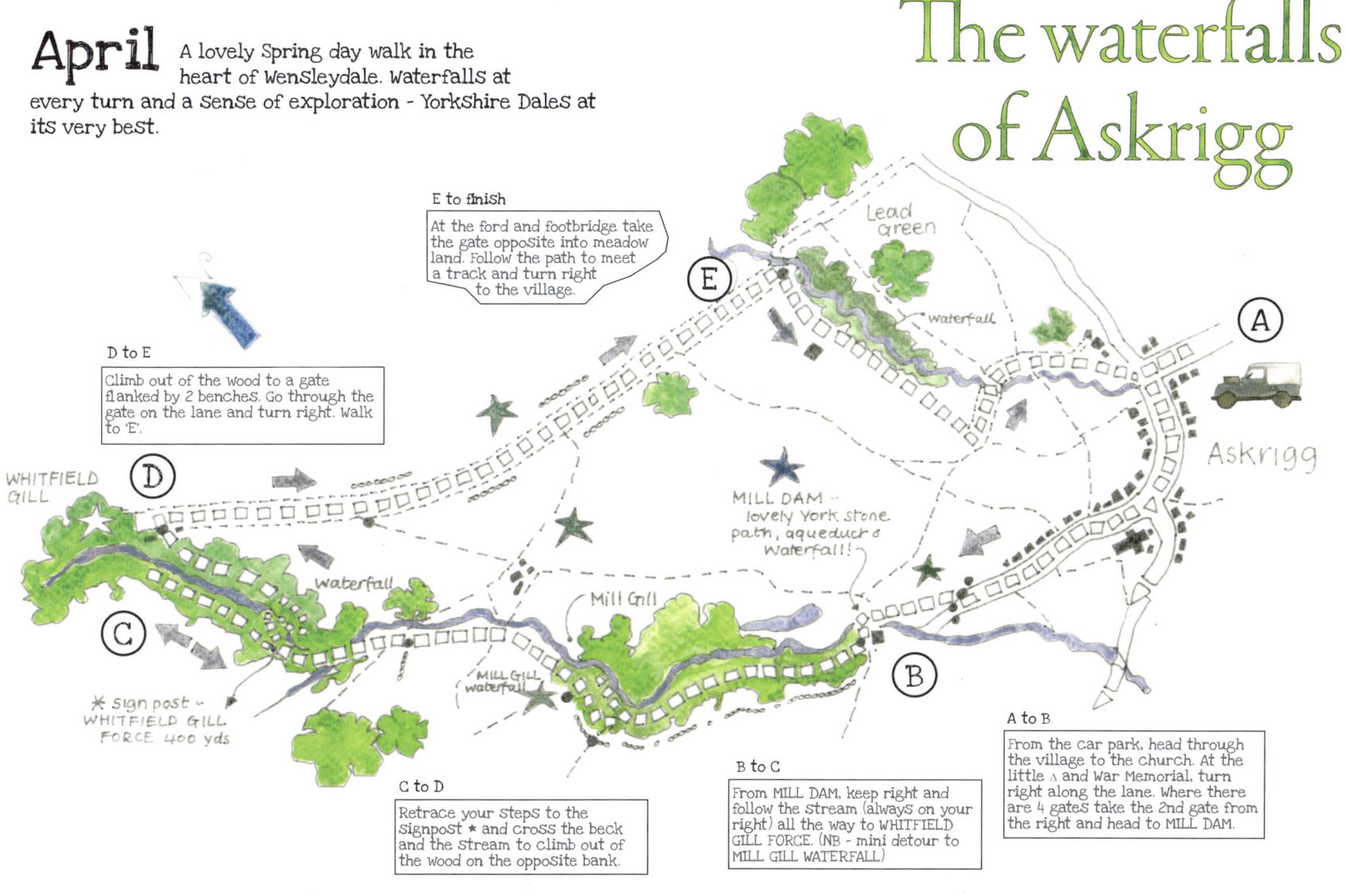

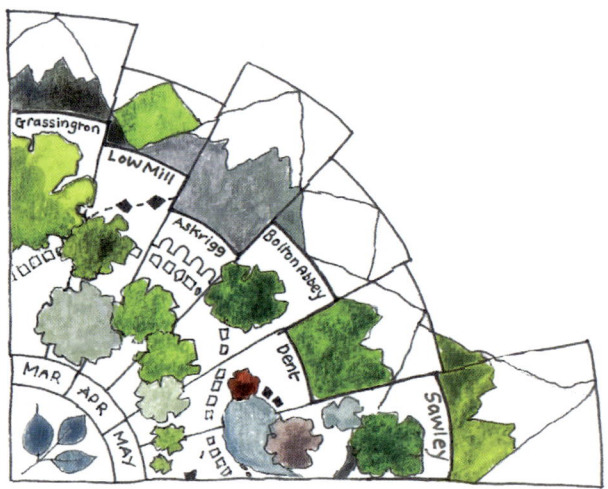

Bolton Abbey

 Distance 8.5 k / 5¼ miles
Time 2 to 3 hrs
Ascent 187 m

 Park / start of walk
Cavendish Pavilion
Bolton Abbey Estate
Skipton
BD23 6AN

i Useful info

To note - it's free to park at Cavendish Pavilion if you are a member. £15 per car for non members. More info at www.boltonabbey.com

A reminder of what you get for your entry ... very easy parking on the picnic -by -your -car riverside field. Excellent facilities ... loos, café and shop. Plus other times of year the estate put on trails for children to follow ... Easter /Christmas /Halloween etc. And... Come April and May Bluebell heaven!

 Your best map
Map of Yorkshire Dales - Southern & Western Areas
Whernside, Ingleborough & Pen-y-ghent
OL2 1:25 000

Our second visit to the environs of Bolton Abbey.
This is another walk I save for late April / early May every year.
Parking at the Cavendish Pavilion (easy parking, café, loos and gift shop) our path heads north towards Barden Bridge.
A very easy walk to navigate of mainly gentle undulations. Our walk takes you through the woodlands of the Devonshire estate with wild bluebells almost every step of the way.
As said on our previous walk, the pavilion, immediate woods and Abbey are a bit of a honey pot, but once again when we leave the car park and coffee shop the walk becomes much quieter.
The secrets of our bluebell laden woods is well and truly out!
The opportunity of easy parking and those wishing to picnic at the riverside is very easy for many to access. But as said, your initial shock of the weekend crowds will soon be left behind once you step out on your walk.
There is an easy short cut at the Victorian castleated bridge that you pass, making our walk a fantastic starter walk for young families ... with perhaps the treat of a picnic at the end.
I feel the environs of Bolton Abbey and this very short window of bluebells is worth a visit every day to witness our phenomena.
It draws me back year after year. I hope it finds a place in your heart as it is very firmly planted in ours.

- **The wonders of Dentdale - Dent**
- **Outstanding Natural Beauty of Eavestone Lake - Sawley & Eavestone**

May is my favourite month. Warmer days, every tree and flower racing to look their best and so, so pretty!

As a young girl I moved from the West Riding to our beautiful city of York. I was in awe of the abundance of stunning pink cherry blossom and the contrasting chalky greens of the whitebeams. My lifelong love of colour in nature was born and the rest is history, as they say!

Our walks take us to the World Heritage sites of Upper Swaledale and the very secret Eavestone. Here we are deep into the Dales - winding, narrow roads through every village along the way with great walks to offer in every direction. Your drive will reward you with fields flush with yellow buttercups and the trees bursting with lush, new growth. Mother Nature in all her finery!

Your visit to Eavestone is the opposite of your water cooler walk! This gem is just for us...you are sworn to secrecy!

Dent

Distance 6 k / 3¾ miles
Allow time 2 hrs
Ascent 162 m

Where to park
Dent Village car park
Laning
Dent
LA10 5QJ

i Useful info

www.kirkbylonsdale.co.uk

Your best map
Ordnance Survey
Map of Yorkshire Dales - Southern & Western Areas
Whernside, Ingleborough & Pen-y-ghent
OL2 1:25 000

O ur walk from the lovely village of Dent is a meadow ramble - easy to navigate and lots of diversity along the way.

Dent is a quintessential Dales village which boasts of being in the Yorkshire Dales National Park but it's actually in Cumbria!

The lovely winding cobbled streets, white-washed cottages and a host of good pubs, cafés and shops complete the scene.

Dent has its own railway station although to say it's in Dent is a little bit of a stretch!

Our walk is lovely at any time of year but the winter months can make Dent and the narrow remote roads a challenge in adverse weather. My favourites are the dandelion heaven of April, the full spring glories of May and the late summer months where a camp over is just a super getaway bank holiday treat.

The wonders of Dentdale

May A great summer destination to camp or caravan in beautiful DENTDALE. A plethora of walks are on offer with a good pub and village store to keep everyone fed and watered. This is a favourite family walk following meadow paths and the famous DALES WAY. Dent is a gem of the YORKSHIRE DALES NATIONAL PARK even though it is in Cumbria!

St Andrew's Church, Dent

A to B
From the church, take the lane to SLACK. Look out for a drive on your right to take you steeply uphill. A field path soon strikes off left to take you over the fields.

B to C
From your birds-eye view of DENT, follow the path over the fields, stiles and bridges to COVENTREE. Use the yellow markers to navigate around WEST BANKS, EAST BANKS and NEAR HELKS.

C to D
At COVENTREE, bear left to join the road - turning right towards SLACK. A short walk on the lane brings you to PEACOCK HILL, where a path is going to cross your lane. Turn left here, down the hill to SCOW.

NB: Your path crosses tumbledown walls and enters the wood on your right.

D to E
Go down the hill and around the farmhouse at SCOW. The path is sketchy but keep the wood and the beck to your right. Head for the road at BRIDGE END.

E to F
At BRIDGE END cross the road and take the path to the left of a beck. A clear path following the beck and RIVER DEE takes you all the way to the playing fields of DENT village.

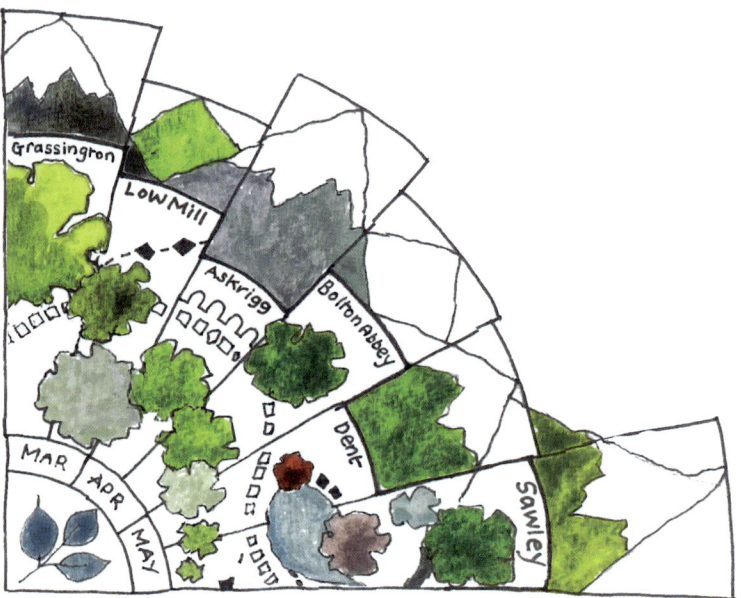

10

Sawley & Eavestone

Distance 9 k / 5½ miles
Time 3 hrs
Ascent 232 m

Park at the village green
The Parish Rooms
Sawley
HG4 3EQ

Useful info

www.yorkshiredales.co.uk/villages/muker/

Your best map

Ordnance Survey
Map of Nidderdale
Fountains Abbey, Ripon & Pateley Bridge
298 1:25 000

Our walk from Sawley takes us on a meander around the countryside and environs of Eavestone and Grantley.

Sawley village (and our walk) falls in the Nidderdale area of outstanding natural beauty - delivering exactly that!

Your walk includes a lake, river, meadows, a brief encounter with a very dark wood and pretty villages.

This walk is an absolute favourite because it is so intimate and varied. It illustrates my thoughts beautifully that some of the best walks are to be found outside the National Parks … full of diversity and away from the crowds! But our walk comes with a caveat …sssh …you must keep it secret!

It's undoubted beauty is the priceless peace and tranquility you will find by the lake.

Take care to follow your trusty OS map lovely walkers - there are many other paths (for you to try another day!). The village boasts a good pub at The Sawley Arms.

May

Come the lovely warmer days of late spring and the world races away to the Dales and the moors, this absolute gem of a walk has everything including peace & quiet! Our walk takes us to the gorgeous EAVESTONE LAKE, and the environs of GRANTLEY HALL. But remember - shh! once again this one is just for you.

Outstanding natural beauty of Eavestone Lake

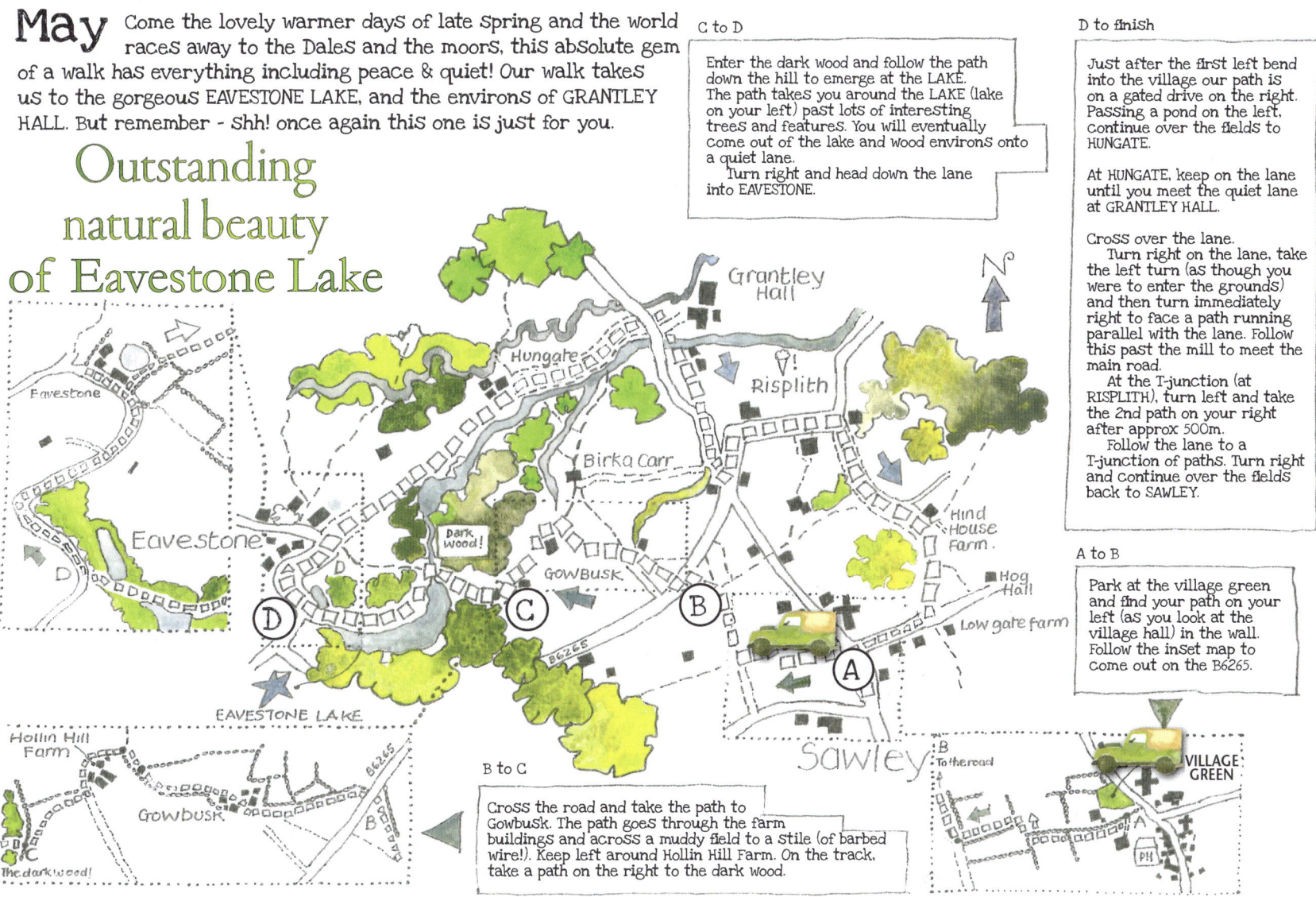

C to D

Enter the dark wood and follow the path down the hill to emerge at the LAKE. The path takes you around the LAKE (lake on your left) past lots of interesting trees and features. You will eventually come out of the lake and wood environs onto a quiet lane.

Turn right and head down the lane into EAVESTONE.

D to finish

Just after the first left bend into the village our path is on a gated drive on the right. Passing a pond on the left, continue over the fields to HUNGATE.

At HUNGATE, keep on the lane until you meet the quiet lane at GRANTLEY HALL.

Cross over the lane.

Turn right on the lane, take the left turn (as though you were to enter the grounds) and then turn immediately right to face a path running parallel with the lane. Follow this past the mill to meet the main road.

At the T-junction (at RISPLITH), turn left and take the 2nd path on your right after approx 500m.

Follow the lane to a T-junction of paths. Turn right and continue over the fields back to SAWLEY.

A to B

Park at the village green and find your path on your left (as you look at the village hall) in the wall. Follow the inset map to come out on the B6265.

B to C

Cross the road and take the path to Gowbusk. The path goes through the farm buildings and across a muddy field to a stile (of barbed wire!). Keep left around Hollin Hill Farm. On the track, take a path on the right to the dark wood.

- # World Heritage Wonders of Swaledale - Muker & Ivelet
- # Up and Over Kisdon Fell - Keld & Muker

The most perfect month for walking, June affords us good weather, jaw dropping flower meadows and long and lovely daylight. All our planets in a line!

June, on a more personal note, brings me lovely memories of my late father. From my earliest memories he would love to explain the summer solstice to me. His love of the universe and the natural world around us was infectious and I most certainly shared his enthusiasm.

I was also born upon the solstice and many times my birthday fell upon Fathers Day. It really was our day. And so every year I always set the alarm to welcome in the longest day wherever I am in the world. The morning hush before the dawn chorus is truly special, the best of mindfulness, a time for gratitude and, for me, a time to thank the universe for my lovely dad.

To camp over in Swaledale for the magic of Midsummer's Day is a real treat. Just to be there in the World Heritage flower meadows, experiencing the daybreak is priceless.

From Ivelet to Muker.

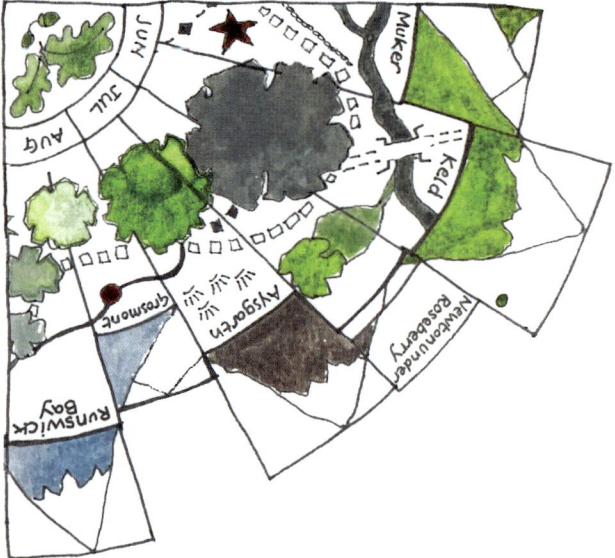

11

Muker & Ivelet

Distance 8 k / 5 miles
Time allow 2 to 3 hrs
Ascent 146 m

Where to park
Public car park Muker
Guning Lane
Muker
DL11 6QG

i Useful info

To note on the birdies
There are some super ground nesting birds to see in our late Spring window... look out for pied and grey wagtail, dipper, common sandpiper and oystercatcher.

Your best map

Map of Yorkshire Dales - Northern & Central Areas
Wensleydale & Swaledale
OL30 1:25 000

Our walk starts in the charming village of Muker in upper Swaledale. Muker boasts a good pub - the Farmers Arms, shop, café and a lovely campsite at Usha Gap. The walk takes you down an ancient Yorkstone path to the river and then an easy riverside navigation to Ivelet and return.

And thus I would say around the middle of the month the floral display will be at its zenith, should you wish to fine tune your experience!

No matter how tempted you are to leave the path to maybe get 'that picture'...just resist! ...when it says it's single file you will be the one who does just that!

You can become quite evangelical about it! Mother Nature is thanking you for being her angel!

This is probably the easiest of our three walks. Extremely easy to navigate by simply following the river to Ivelet with a fantastic field to field stroll home.

So ...Your highlights ...There is a lovely bridge to view at Ivelet, a Birds-Eye view of Muker on your return, a perfect place to paddle at the footbridge and ... those meadow flowers on the Yorkstone path ... wow just wow.

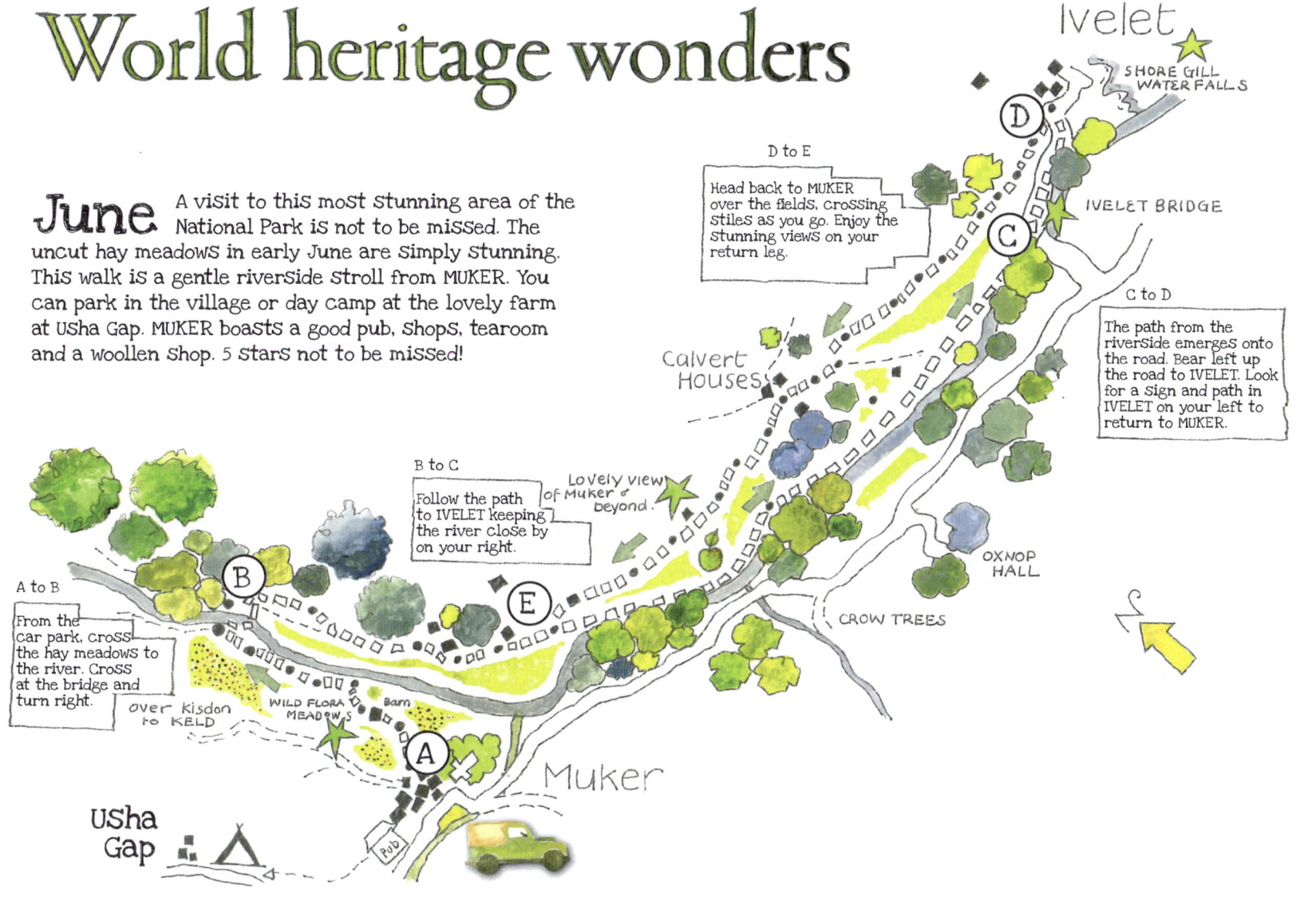

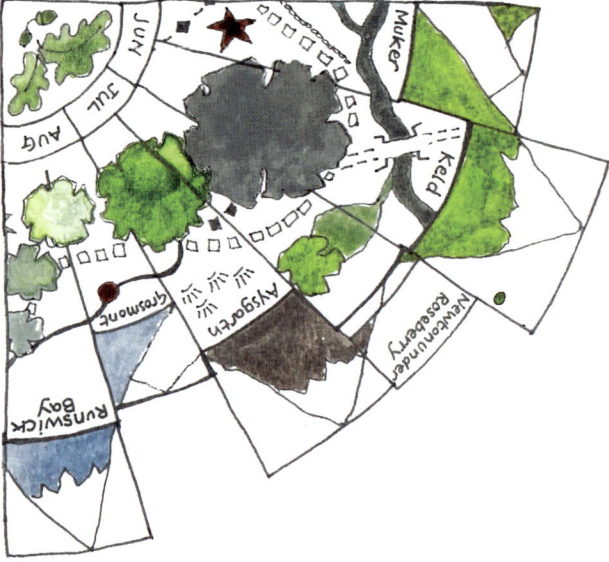

Keld & Muker

Distance 8.5 k / 5¼ miles
Time allow 2 to 3 hrs
Ascent 146 m

Our walk in Upper Swaledale at this most wonderful time of year. This time your last peek at those hay meadows and some extra treats in store!

Our walk takes us up and over mighty Kisdon Fell with all the rewards of fantastic views on all sides. Your return is a riverside ramble all the way back to Keld - easy to follow - full of colour - with a flourish of waterfalls at Keld for you to explore.

There are pubs, shops and facilities at Muker with a shop and pub at Keld.

As we've touched on in these Summer Swaledale walks ... it can all get a little busy but careful planning and common sense to avoid the super busy times will very much enhance your visit.

Where to park
The public car park at Keld
Park Lodge
Keld
DL11 6LJ

Or Public car park Muker
Guning Lane
Muker
DL11 6QG

i Useful info

https://www.yorkshiredales.co.uk/villages/muker/

Your best map

Map of Yorkshire Dales - Northern & Central Areas
Wensleydale & Swaledale
OL30 1:25 000

Up and over Kisdon Fell

June Another chance to catch the stunning wild flower meadows of UPPER SWALEDALE. Our walk starts in Keld and takes you up and over mighty Kisdon Fell. Keld boasts many waterfalls and is the famous meeting place of the Coast to Coast and Pennine Way. Enjoy the meadows lovely walkers but remember SINGLE FILE at All TIMES!

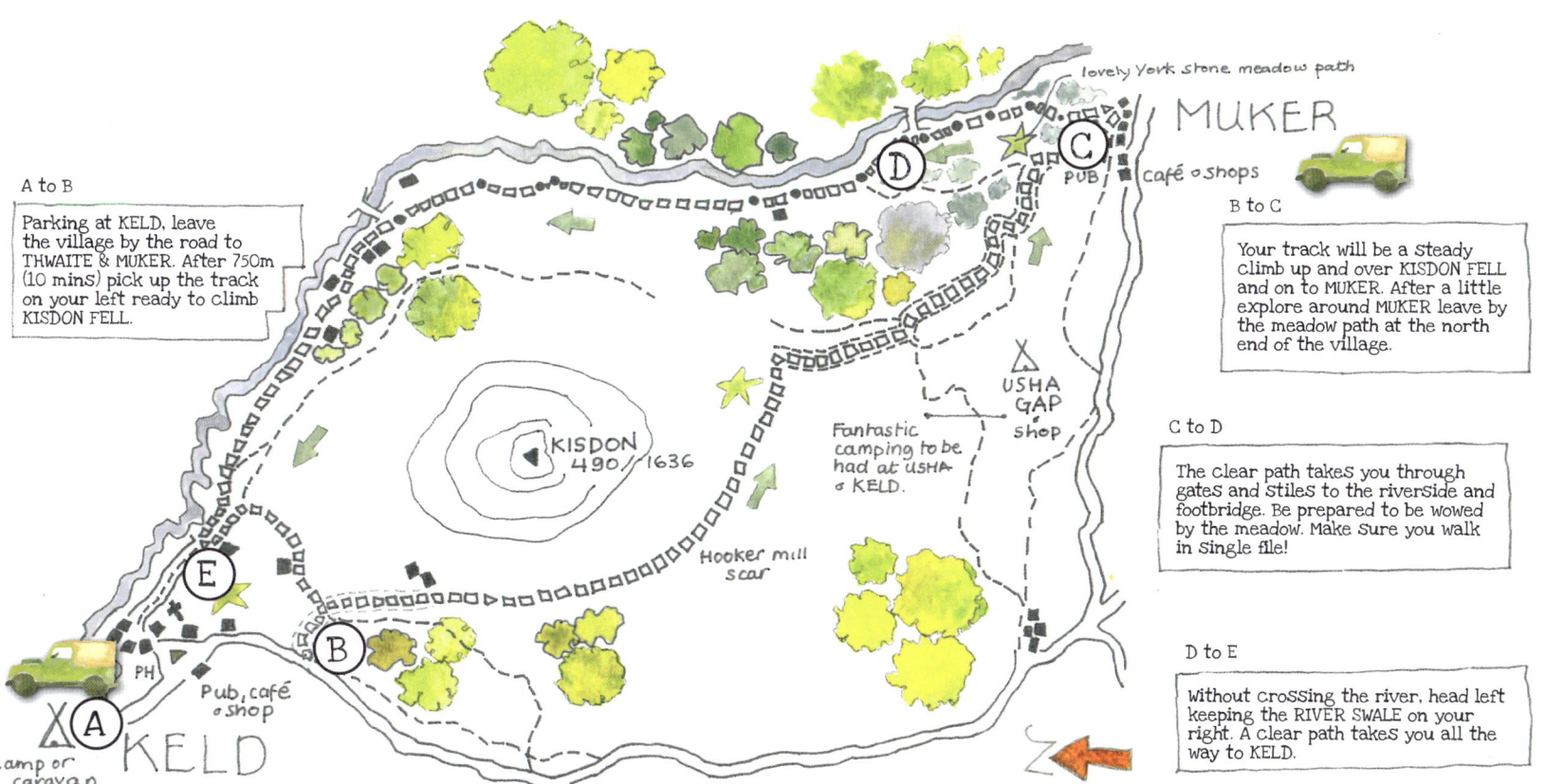

A to B
Parking at KELD, leave the village by the road to THWAITE & MUKER. After 750m (10 mins) pick up the track on your left ready to climb KISDON FELL.

B to C
Your track will be a steady climb up and over KISDON FELL and on to MUKER. After a little explore around MUKER leave by the meadow path at the north end of the village.

C to D
The clear path takes you through gates and stiles to the riverside and footbridge. Be prepared to be wowed by the meadow. Make sure you walk in Single file!

D to E
Without crossing the river, head left keeping the RIVER SWALE on your right. A clear path takes you all the way to KELD.

45

- # Yorkshire Matterhorn - Newton under Roseberry
- # The Magic of Aysgarth Falls - Aysgarth & West Burton

July can be a double-edged sword. The children on school holidays will make those honey pots even busier but adversely everything is open and in full swing.

If you have children to entertain I can't recommend enough the Heritage Railways at the Keighley & Worth Valley (see walk 24) and North York Moors at Goathland (see walk 15). Our seaside villages hug the Cleveland Way and so walks and fun are easily found.

Our choice of walks offer climbs and adventure and may help you get older children off the sofa!

The heat of the summer is not always ideal so we urge you to take all sun precautions and plenty of picnic! July is a month to take our time. A time to sit aloft Roseberry Topping or revisit How Hill (walk 4), the breeze and sunshine on our faces and making the very most of everything summertime.

'The Framed View' Roseberry Topping

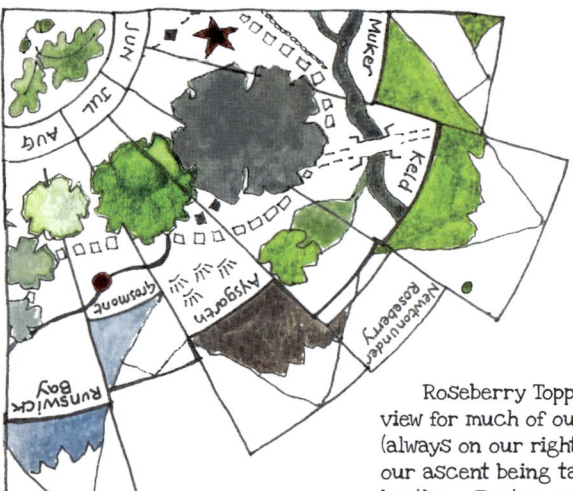

Newton under Roseberry

July fits our chosen walk beautifully... the sunny days of summer casting a glow on the mountain and surrounding woods. A popular honey pot in the school holidays (a climb with lofty views that is extremely accessible) ...but our ramble around the hill is a little quieter.

Our walk starts at the roadside car park beneath Roseberry Topping. There are good facilities here and a clear lane takes us to the foot of the mountain.

'Quick to climb' visitors will take the direct route up and down but we shall leave them behind and traverse through the lovely Oak laden woodland.

Roseberry Topping stays in view for much of our walk (always on our right !) with our ascent being taken on the heathery Eastern side.

We are afforded lovely moorland views all the way with the perfect 'framed view' at the entrance to Cliff Ridge Wood. Camera at the ready!

The climb to the very top is quick and exhilarating! The National Trust have well cut stone steps for our path heavenward. But! ...as said, our beautiful Roseberry Topping is very popular! You may have to wait your turn for your trig point picture.

However, lovely walker, your peace and quiet will return through the beautiful woods and breezy moorland tracks.

To note: Roseberry is criss crossed with many, many paths. I have chosen the clearest routes that are all well sign posted.

Our Yorkshire Matterhorn is one for the tick list for sure.

Distance 6.5 k / 4 miles
Time allow 2 to 3 hrs
Ascent 371 m

Where to park
White Croft
Newton Under Roseberry car park
Just off A173
Middlesbrough
TS9 6QR

i Useful info

Your best map

OS Explorer
OL26 North York Moors western Area

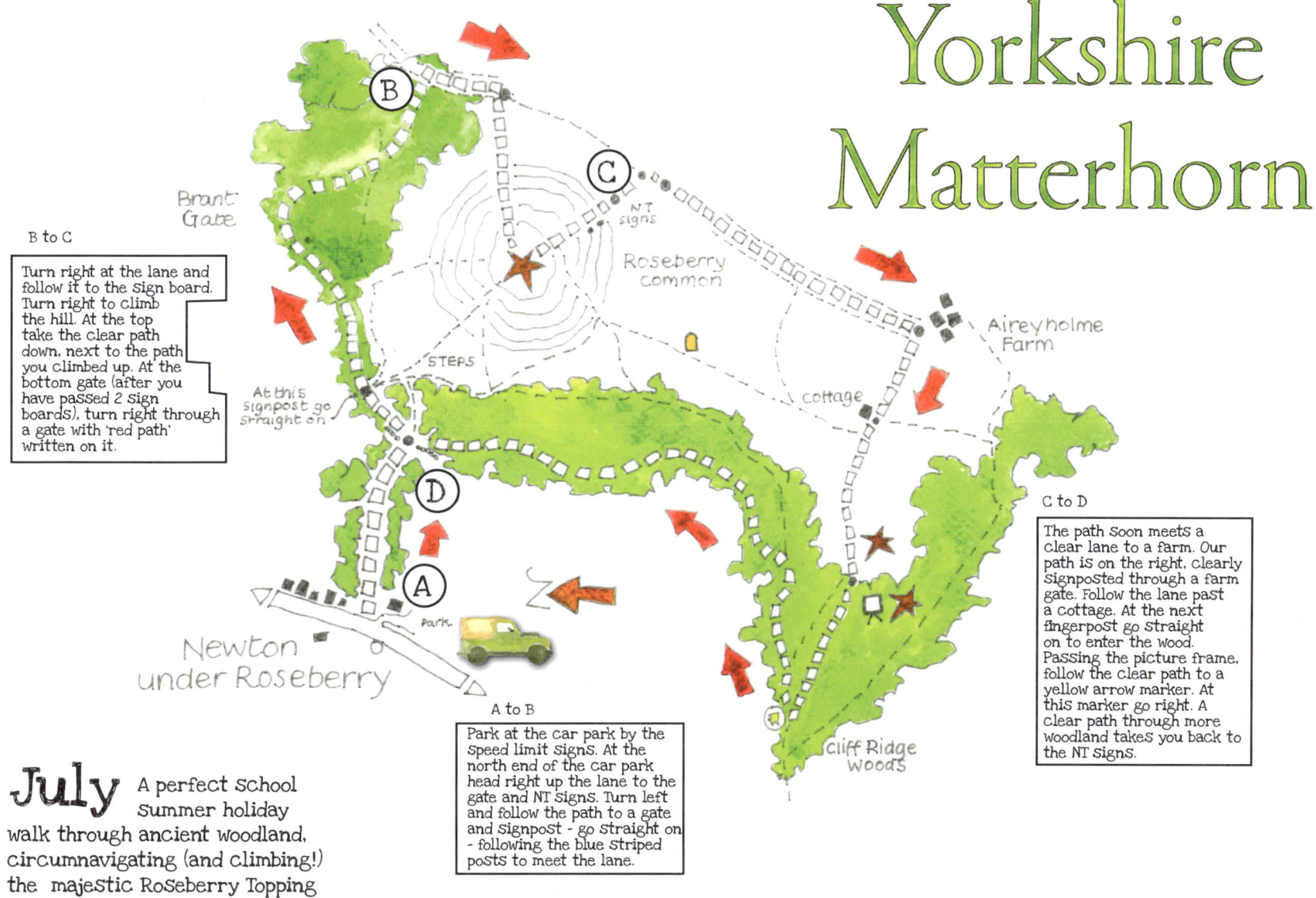

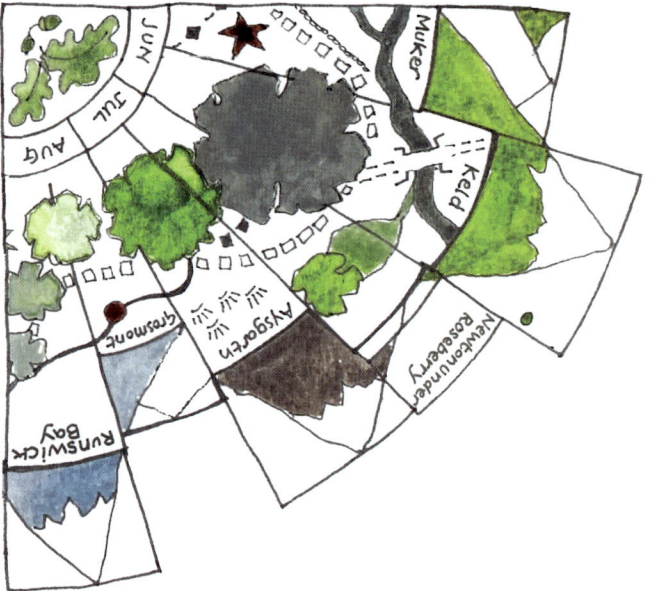

14

Aysgarth & West Burton

 Distance 7 k / 4½ miles
Allow time 2 to 2½ hrs
Ascent 166 m

 Start & Where to park

Aysgarth Falls
National Park Visitor Centre
Aysgarth
DL8 3TH

This is an amazing walk around the environs of Aysgarth and West Burton.

Our walk takes you through a lovely churchyard, waterfalls, meadows and woodland.

The Aysgarth National Park visitor centre has a café, information and loos alongside easy parking.

A gentle walk for Summer... take a picnic to enjoy those lower falls ... simply stunning! ... for an extra treat you could finish your walk with a visit to the upper falls (knowing you've just experienced the lower falls all to yourself !).

Other treats along the way ... look out for a gorgeous little set of steps in the wall at West Burton and the noisy birds in the tiny wood at point C.

Our walk is mainly gently undulating but there is a sharp pull up the hill to Flattlands.

But a little note to remember ... do come again in late April early May ... your secret wood at Flattlands will be full of bluebells and your 'crow wood' thick with intoxicating garlic in full flower.

i Useful info

www.yorkshiredales.org.uk/places/aysgarth_falls_national_park_centre

 Your best map

Map of Yorkshire Dales - Northern & Central Areas
Wensleydale & Swaledale
OL30 1:25 000

The magic of Aysgarth Falls

A to B
Park at the visitor centre and leave the car park by the bottom path - heading for the river. Leaving the crowds to the upper force, instead cross the bridge, past the MILL, taking the steps up to the church.

B to C
Leave the churchyard by a gate to cross a field to a small wood. Keeping the river and falls on your left, simply follow the path to the main road at HESTHOLME BRIDGE.

C to D
At the main road, turn left for just a few metres. Cross the road with great care to enter the wood (on the other side of the road). A path through the wood brings you to a minor road. Turn right to cross over to a gate that takes you over the fields to WEST BURTON.

D to E
In the heart of WEST BURTON head north on the road, keeping left.

E to F to G
From WEST BURTON, look out for a path on the left by the wall to save you walking on the road. At the junction look for a gate and take the path straight up the steep bank.

G to H
The path bears left and then right towards FLATTLANDS. At a crossroad of paths take the right path to a tiny wood.

H to finish
Enter the wood and bear left to leave the wood at the top. The path now heads back to the main road, and thus the church for you to navigate your return leg.

July A lovely walk at any time of the year full of secret surprises. Leave the crowds who will head for the famous Upper falls and treat yourself to having the middle and lower falls all in wonderful seclusion. West Burton is a gem and do come again in early May to see the bluebell wood at Flattlands. Enjoy!

- Full Steam Ahead on the North York Moors - Goathland, Beck Hole & Grosmont
- Sandcastles and Hobgoblins - Runswick Bay

August is a time to head to the Moors. The flush of purple heather stretching out like an endless sea conjures up memories of our childhood car journeys to Whitby passing those famous 'golf balls'.

We are spoilt for choice in Yorkshire for finding moorland magic; the walks above the Cow & Calf Rocks at Ilkley, Merryfield Mines at Pately Bridge, the shapely hills of Hawnby, and the walk from Helmsley to Rievaulx are all favourites. We can plan those for another day! But for our collection I've chosen a family favourite - to walk the steam heritage line of the North Yorkshire Moors Railway and our most loved seaside haunt of Runswick Bay.

Like July we can expect everything up and running and open for business. With the railway in full steam there is much to see and plenty of chances to catch a return ride home!

For our seaside day, the tiny car park at Runswick is supplemented by a lovely open field on the cliff top. The stress of finding somewhere to park is taken from us and a grand day out at the seaside awaits.

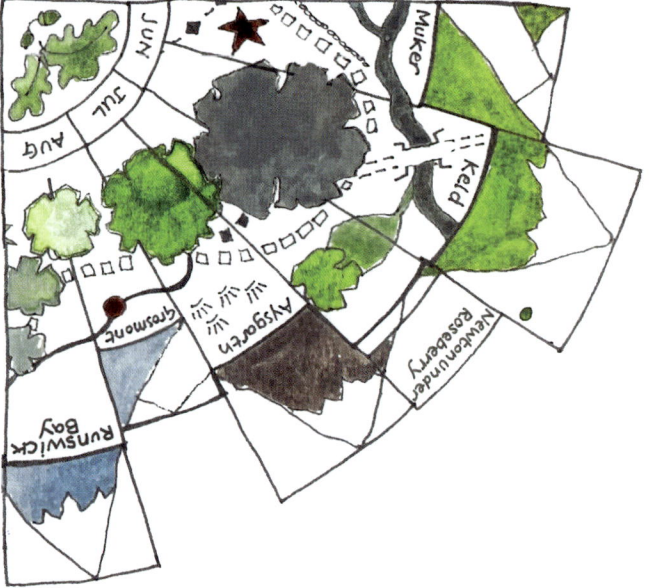

Goathland, Beck Hole & Grosmont

Distance 6 k / 3¾ miles (linear walk)
Allow time 2 to 2.5 hrs
Ascent 166 m

Where to park / start of walk
Ample parking at
Goathland car park
Beck Hole Road
YO22 5LZ

 Useful info

https://www.nymr.co.uk

Your best map

Ordnance Survey
Map of North York Moors - Eastern area
OL27 1:25 000

Grosmont is a lovely village centred around the Heritage North Yorkshire Moors Railway. The station, the engine sheds, shops, pub and cafés make Grosmont a great afternoon out in its own right. Your walk from Goathland keeps you in close proximity to the line with lots of opportunity to experience the steam locos going at full steam! There are engine sheds to explore and you'll be treated to a fantastic birds-eye view of Grosmont right at the end of your walk. The stations are a heritage delight and well run and staffed by volunteers. Do check times of trains if you plan to ride the return journey (their website below).

Do remember busier times - weekends and children's school holidays work in your favour as more trains will be running and thus more to see. Our walk at any time of the year is never over busy.

All aboard!

Full steam ahead on the North York Moors

August

A lovely ride over the NORTH YORK MOORS to see the Heather in full bloom and experience the NYMR (The North Yorkshire Moors Railway) in full steam! A fantastic walk for smaller children with lots to see and the promise of the return journey by locomotion!

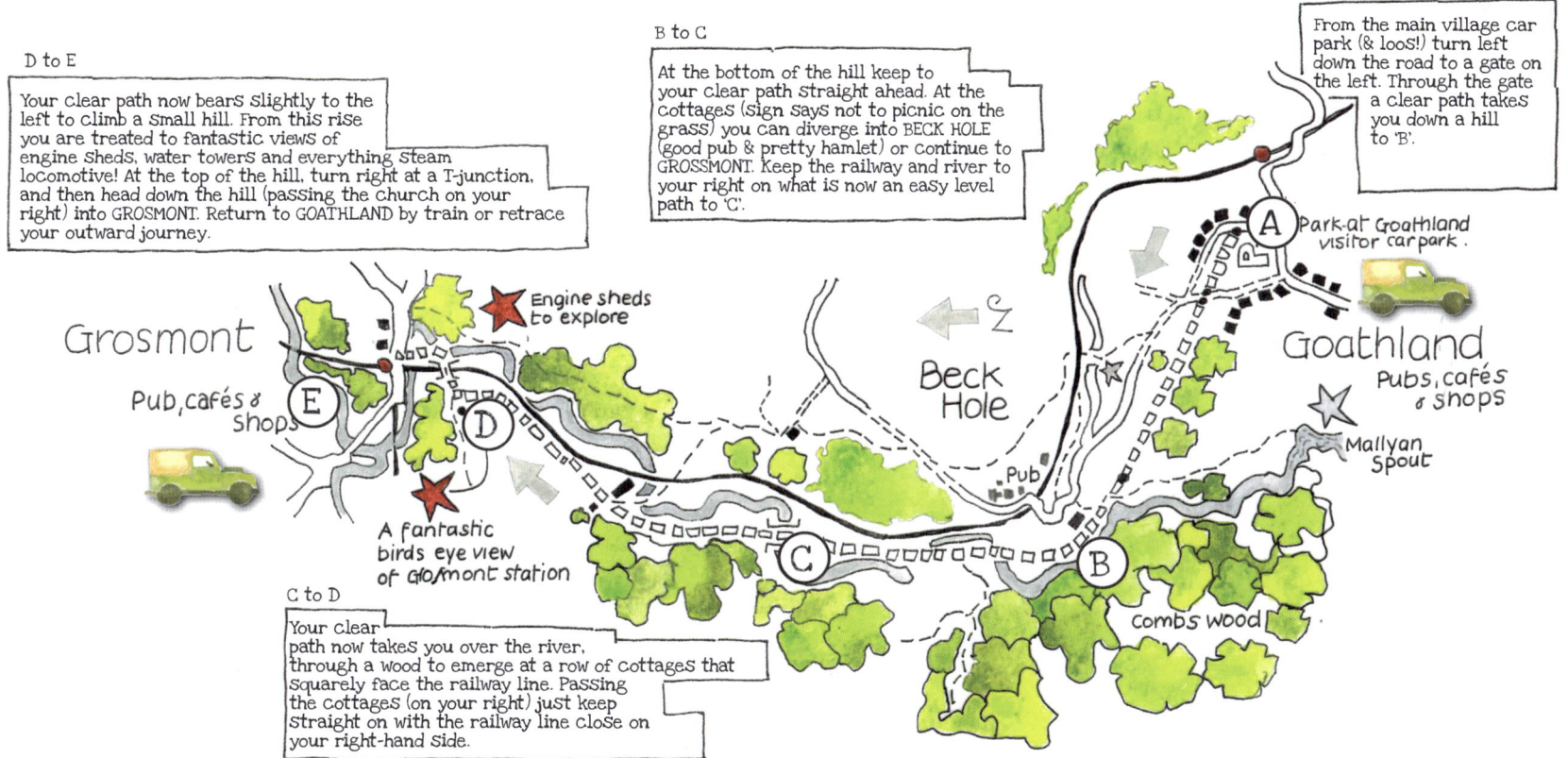

A to B
From the main village car park (& loos!) turn left down the road to a gate on the left. Through the gate a clear path takes you down a hill to 'B'.

B to C
At the bottom of the hill keep to your clear path straight ahead. At the cottages (sign says not to picnic on the grass) you can diverge into BECK HOLE (good pub & pretty hamlet) or continue to GROSMONT. Keep the railway and river to your right on what is now an easy level path to 'C'.

C to D
Your clear path now takes you over the river, through a wood to emerge at a row of cottages that squarely face the railway line. Passing the cottages (on your right) just keep straight on with the railway line close on your right-hand side.

D to E
Your clear path now bears slightly to the left to climb a small hill. From this rise you are treated to fantastic views of engine sheds, water towers and everything steam locomotive! At the top of the hill, turn right at a T-junction, and then head down the hill (passing the church on your right) into GROSMONT. Return to GOATHLAND by train or retrace your outward journey.

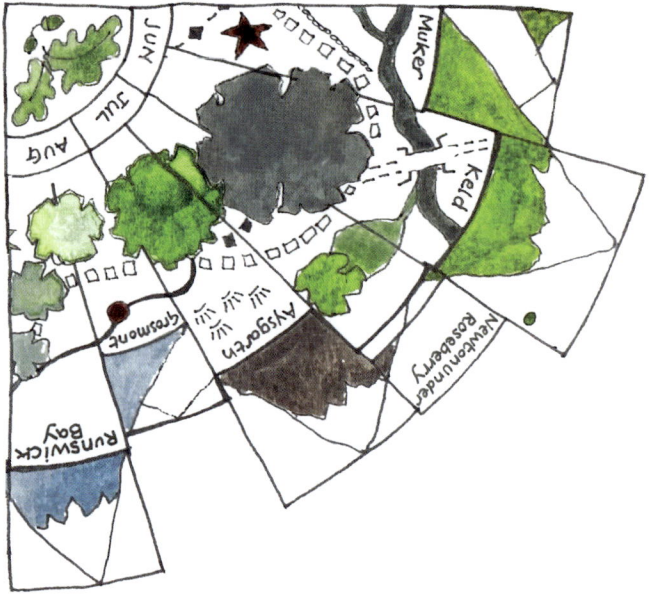

Runswick Bay

Distance 9 k / 5½ miles
Allow 2 to 3 hrs
Ascent 251 m

Start of walk
Bank Bottom car park
Runswick Bay
TS13 5HT

i Useful info

Just google "When is it high tide at Runswick" or Info

www.thebeachguide.co.uk / www.tideschart.com

Your best map

Map of North York Moors - Eastern area
OL27 1:25 000

A few little warnings !

The road down to the beach, the ascent off the beach and the descent back to the beach is steep and slippy in places. The waterfall path after the beach footbridge requires extra care. The clifftop section is unfenced and extra care will be needed for children... lastly... You must check the tides lovely walker, as the sea at high tide may come right up the beach. A there-and-back walk along the disused railway would be your option if tide and time (literally!) are against you.

Come high summer and the beach is calling - Runswick Bay is very much one of our favourite go-to beach destinations.

This lovely little village twixt Whitby and Staithes ticks all the boxes.

It has an award-winning sandy beach, the beach is dog friendly, it has a great overflow parking field in the summer, clean water accreditations, public loos (it's good to know isn't it!) and the options of a 'proper walk' and /or just a stroll on the beach... this completes our full house!

Good fossil hunting is to be had towards Kettleness, there are rock pools and the sand is soft and golden for children to play.

The bay also features interesting caves. The Hob Holes are a series of caves that were made from mining jet. According to folklore they are inhabited by hobgoblins!

The picturesque village of whitewash cottages sits above the lifeboat station. The seasonal café, pub and hotel complete the scene.

Bucket and spade at the ready? Let's go!

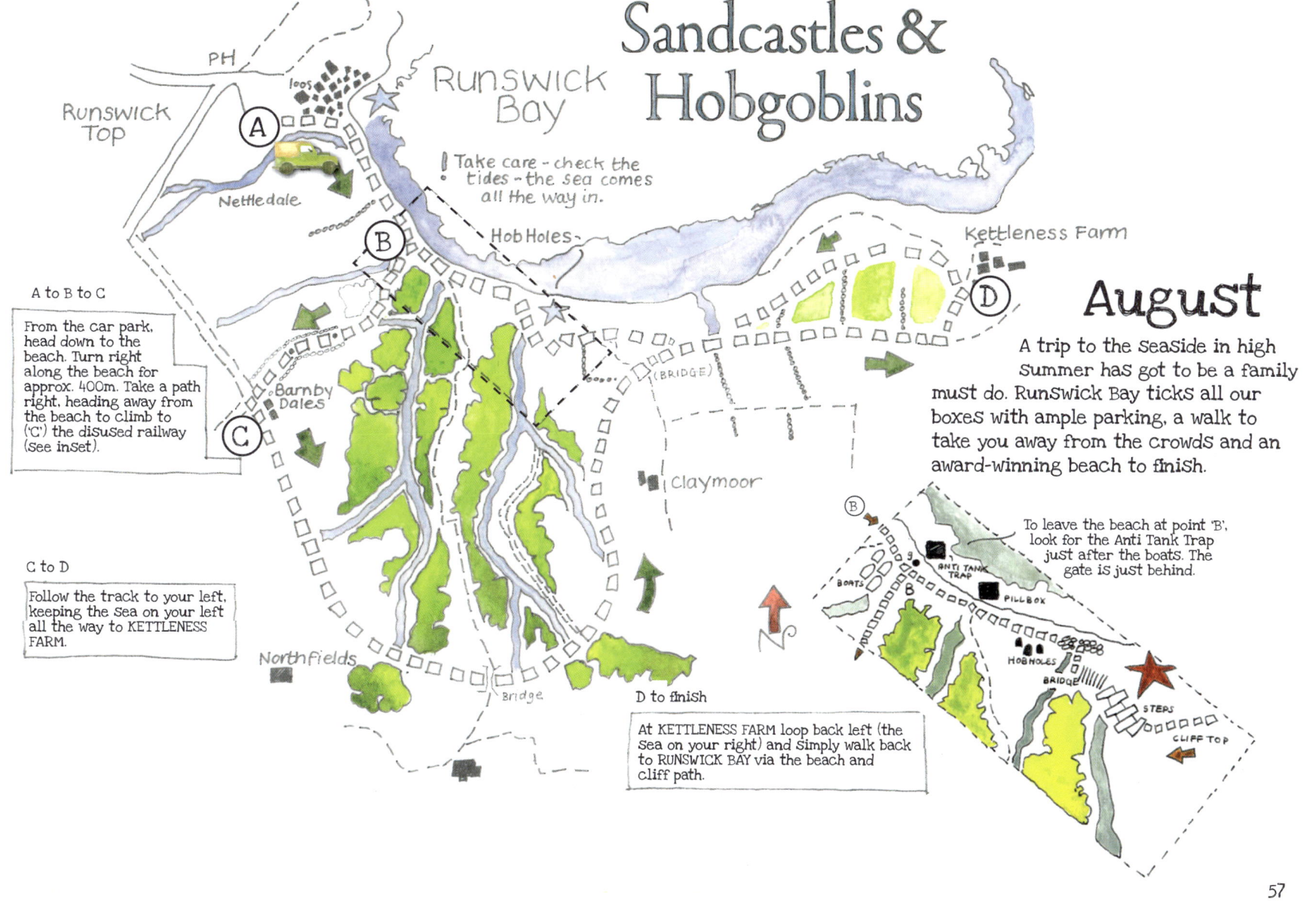

- # The waterfalls of Dent - Dent
- # Secret passageways - Burnsall, Linton & Hebden

Once again we can steal some quieter time as the traditional holiday season comes to an end. The trees are still in leaf and our paths weave through bracken and berry-laden hedgerows. The intoxicating Himalayan balsam is the fragrance of September and the autumn equinox will soon remind us of the shorter daylight hours to come.

Our chosen walks take us for a step out over heathery moors above Dent and to contrast, the lovely enclosed pathways in the environs of Grassington and Burnsall.

Gibson Mill Hebden Bridge

Our month will start all summery and close already embracing the cool of autumn. Many will hang up their boots for the winter ... but not us! Adjusting our attire and being aware of our own limitations, the autumn and winter can all be just as lovely.

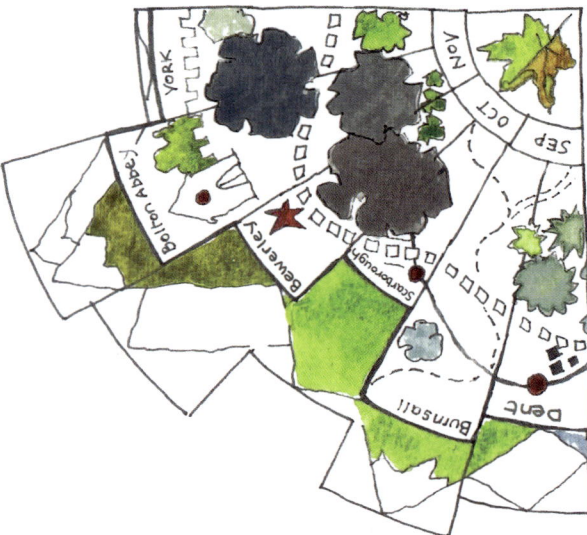

17

Dent

Distance 8 k / 5 miles
Time 2 to 3 hrs
Ascent 300m

Start of walk
Dentdale car park
Laning
LA10 5QJ

 Useful info

Our second visit to lovely Dent ...this time to catch the last of the moorlands in flower and climb to high ground up the waterfalls south of the village.

This is a super walk when you feel you need a nice 'step out'. Once you've climbed to the moorland green lane - it's just a breezy stroll of very easy navigation.

Eventually you must leave the moor and drop down to the intimate environs of the river valley.

Dent really is such a gem. It's isolation gives it a very special away day experience. The village is timeless and has chocolate box appeal that we know will never change.

Famous sons of Dent include geologist Adam Sedgwick and a monument to his life can be found in the village centre.

Dent also lies on the long-distance footpath - the Dales Way.

Other lovely times of year to visit Dent include very early April (Dandelion wonders!) and catch the pretty meadows in flower from May and June ...with many ground nesting birds choosing Dentdale to rear their young.

www.visitlakedistrict.com/explore/dent

Your best map

Ordnance Survey
Map of Yorkshire Dales - Southern & Western Areas
Whernside, Ingleborough & Pen-y-ghent
OL2 1:25 000

The waterfalls of Dent

September
A lovely moorland walk with a wonderful climb alongside a waterfall at the start of your walk. September should give you lots of water in flow, some lovely golden light and a great stride out on the moorland GREEN LANE.

NOTE: Our walk (like all our walks) is lovely at any time but do re-visit this one in early April for dandelion heaven!

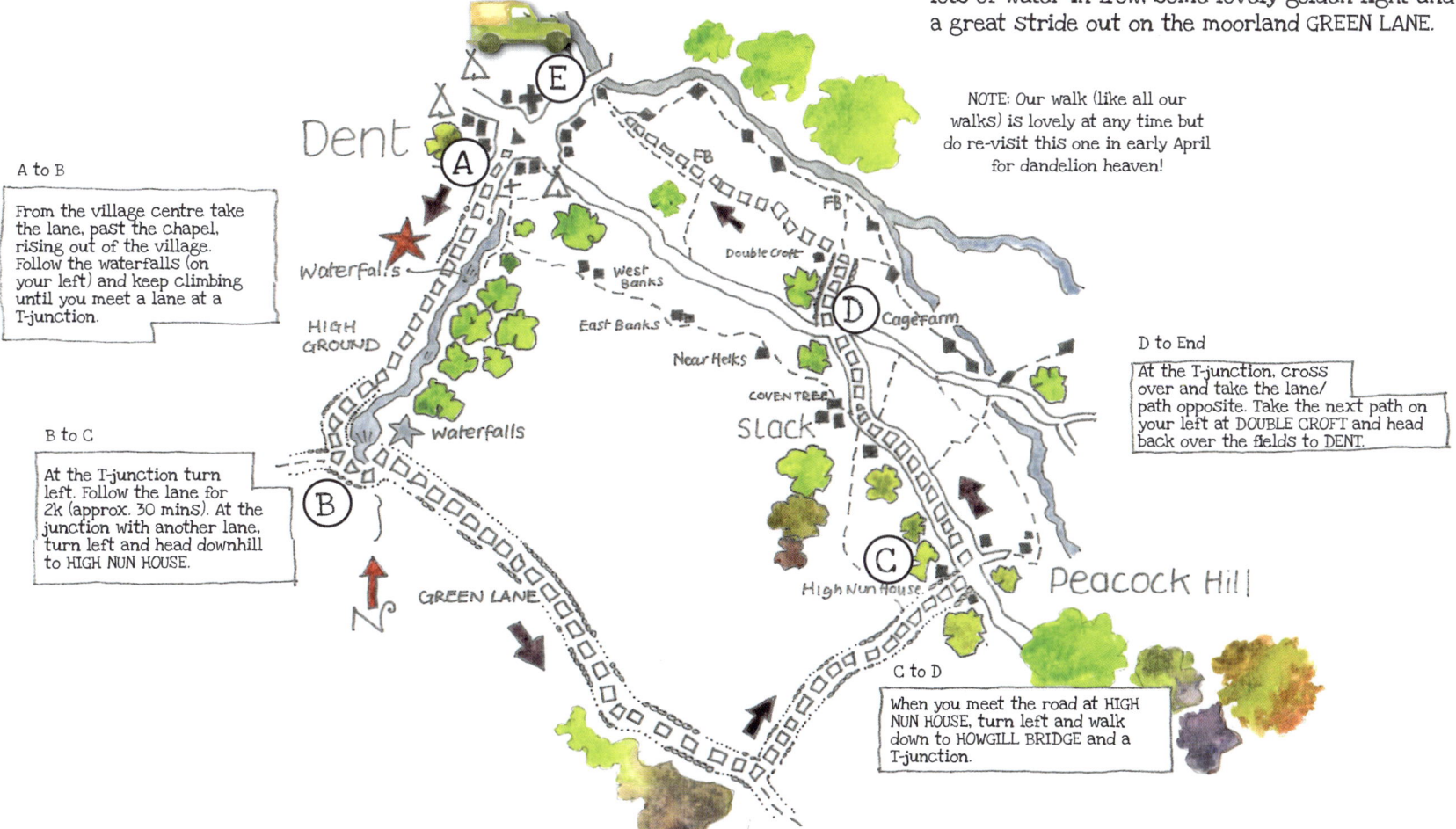

A to B
From the village centre take the lane, past the chapel, rising out of the village. Follow the waterfalls (on your left) and keep climbing until you meet a lane at a T-junction.

B to C
At the T-junction turn left. Follow the lane for 2k (approx. 30 mins). At the junction with another lane, turn left and head downhill to HIGH NUN HOUSE.

C to D
When you meet the road at HIGH NUN HOUSE, turn left and walk down to HOWGILL BRIDGE and a T-junction.

D to End
At the T-junction, cross over and take the lane/path opposite. Take the next path on your left at DOUBLE CROFT and head back over the fields to DENT.

61

18

Burnsall, Linton & Hebden

Distance 10 k / 6 miles
Time 3 to 4 hrs
Ascent 264 m

Start of walk
Burnsall car park
2 Bunkers Hill
Burnsall
BD23 6BS

A lovely ramble around the environs of upper Wharfedale with lots to see and experience.

Our walk once again takes us over the wobbly suspension bridge at Hebden and a chance for the brave to try the stepping stones at Linton!

It's quite a stile hop to leave Burnsall and then a steady climb to the little hamlet of Thorpe.

With Grassington in view our walk to Linton takes us down my favourite 'enclosed field path'.

Once again I think of those who have walked this little path before us down the centuries...Very much an ancient structure to marvel at and treasure.

Our ramble to Hebden is quite a stile hop! ...or you could just walk along the riverside Dales Way.

The Dales Way is an easy to follow option and could be a lovely 'go to' walk in its own right for days when you just need a simple 'no navigation needed' walk.
All in all classic Yorkshire Dales on offer! Enjoy!

 Useful info

www.highlaning.co.uk

Your best map

Ordnance Survey
Map of Yorkshire Dales - Southern & Western Areas
Whernside, Ingleborough & Pen-y-ghent
OL2 1:25 000

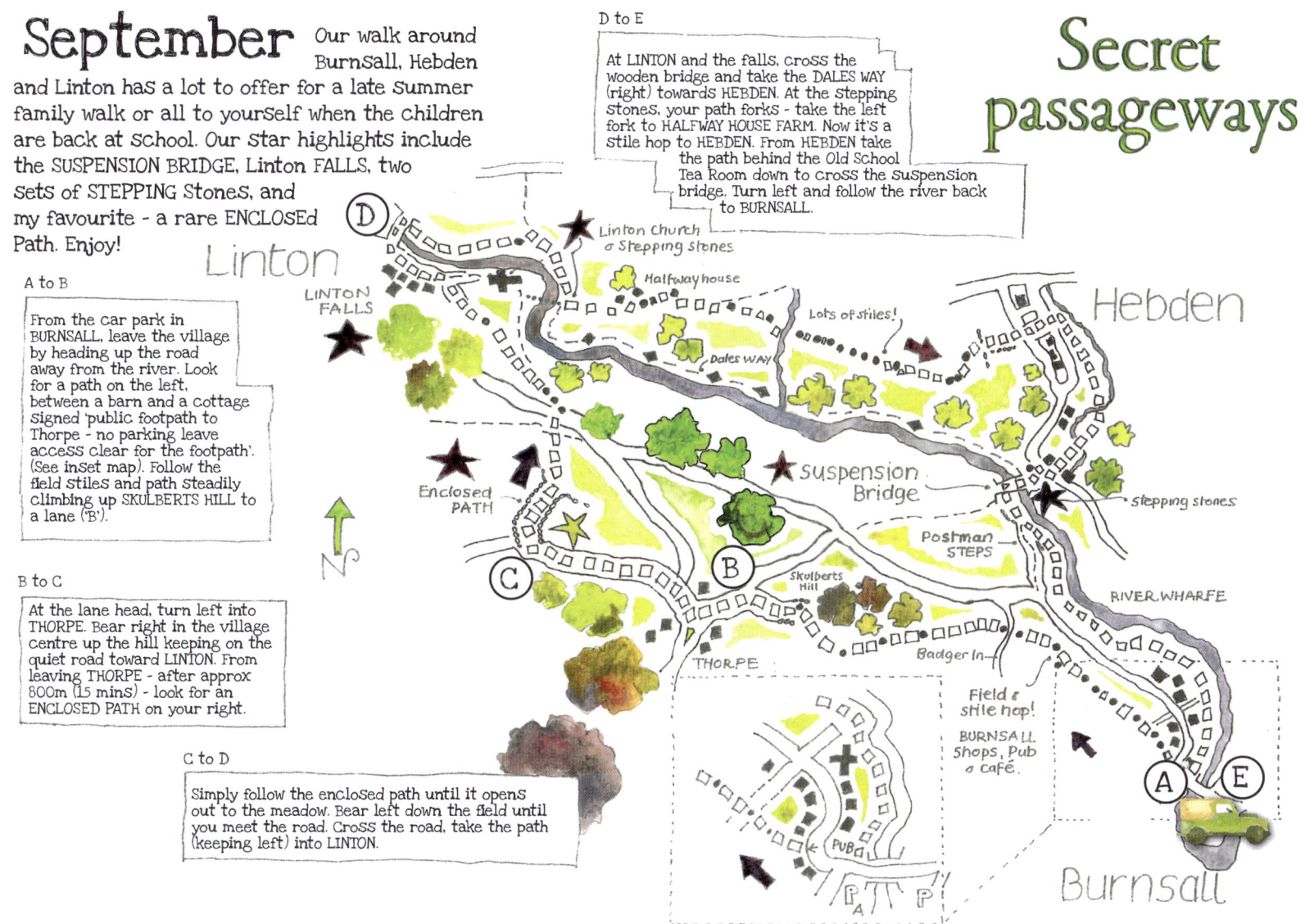

🔴 A walk for small children - Scarborough
🟢 Our little Lake District - Bewerley

For many fellow walkers, autumn is their favourite season. That low, golden light throws us stunning backlit photo opportunities at every turn. Rising mist being burned away by the warming sun can give us glorious rays of sunshine through the tree branches. A photographic extravaganza!

This is a time to once again see the wonder of the world around us. And those colours - reaching their golden zenith around the third week of October.

Our chosen walks could include any of our Yorkshire gorgeous woodlands; Grass Wood, the Devonshire Estate, Hack Fall, Hebden Bridge all come to mind (and I promise I'll write about all of those another day!) but for us we are going to our Little Lake District at Bewerley where you'll find a walk of discovery that we return to year after year.

Away to the coast! Our walk for tiny children is a great one for our grandchildren during half term. Setting good examples we hope, as for us, walking one day becomes their go-to!

Gurnal Dubs Staveley with Hannah & Joe

19

Scarborough

Distance 4 k / 2½ miles
Time 2 hrs
Ascent 66 m

Start of walk
The Sealife centre car park
Scarborough
YO12 6RP

Useful info

Your best map

Ordnance Survey
Scarborough, Bridlington & Flamborough Head
OS Explorer 301

We start our walk at the ample car park at the Sealife centre.

Lovely walker we can take advantage of the October half term whilst although we're at the very end of the season - everything is still open and running. The Sealife centre is very much worth a visit... The seals and penguins are our grandchildren's favourite!

To note there is a café, shop and loos at the centre.

A short climb up the steps in the corner of the car park and you are at the station of the North Bay miniature railway. If you ride the train the open sides give a great sense of speed!

The ride is a lovely treat and our walk even shorter if little legs soon get tired.

Peasholm park and the boating lake offers more refreshments and comfort stops if needed. Here we can sit on the seats, picnic and watch the world go by.

Onwards to the beach (where icecreams, buckets and spades can be purchased) and a steady stroll along the front to be enjoyed to take us home.

This is very much a favourite for us with our very young grandchildren. We can access the whole route with the stroller and little legs get a chance to run, rest, walk and play.

A walk for small children

October A lovely little level starter walk for young children with the option of a ride on the North Bay Railway. The boating lake, the Sealife centre and the beach are our added attractions along the way.

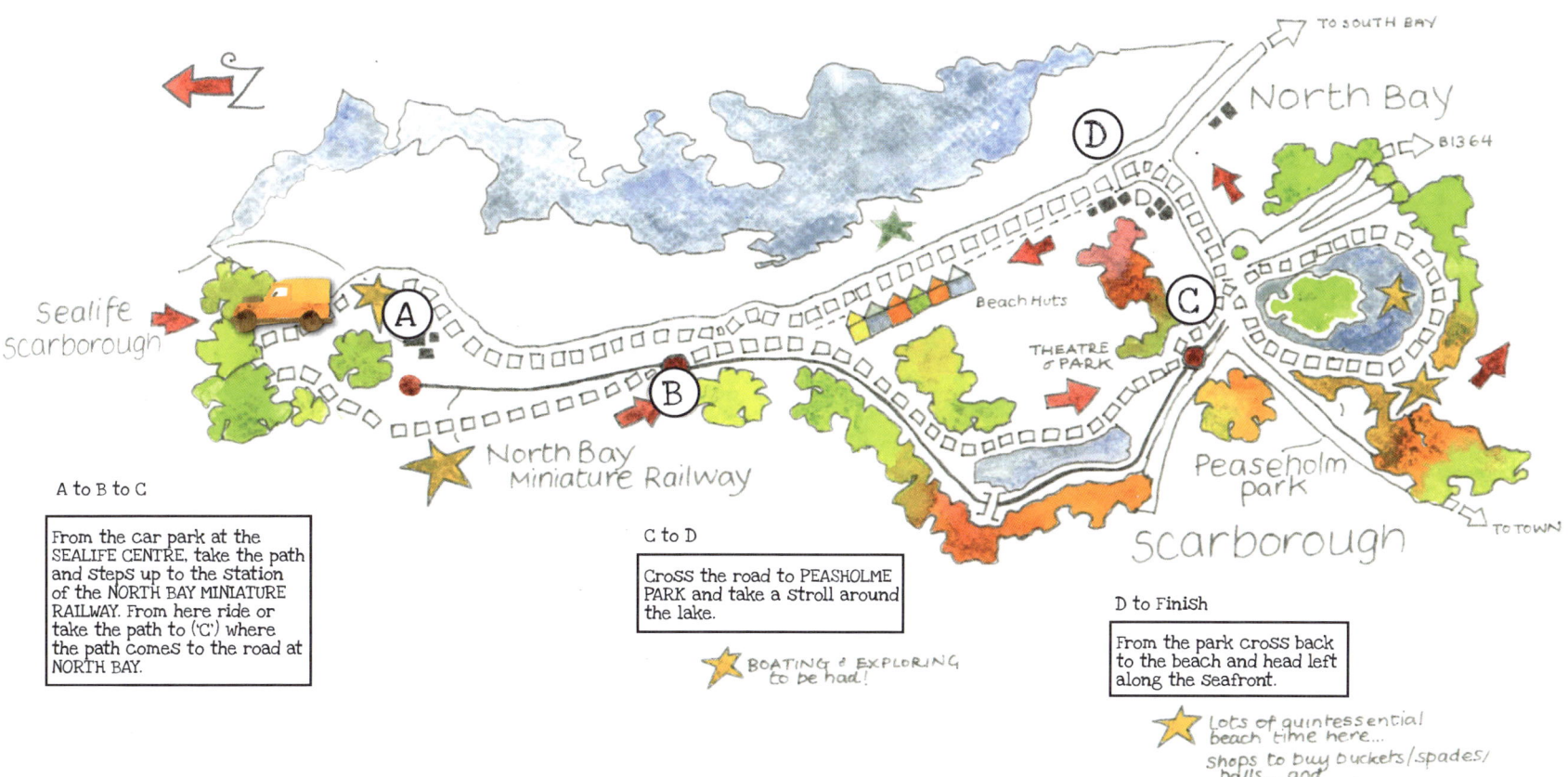

A to B to C

From the car park at the SEALIFE CENTRE, take the path and steps up to the station of the NORTH BAY MINIATURE RAILWAY. From here ride or take the path to ('C') where the path comes to the road at NORTH BAY.

C to D

Cross the road to PEASHOLME PARK and take a stroll around the lake.

⭐ BOATING & EXPLORING to be had!

D to Finish

From the park cross back to the beach and head left along the seafront.

⭐ Lots of quintessential beach time here... shops to buy buckets/spades/balls... and icecream.

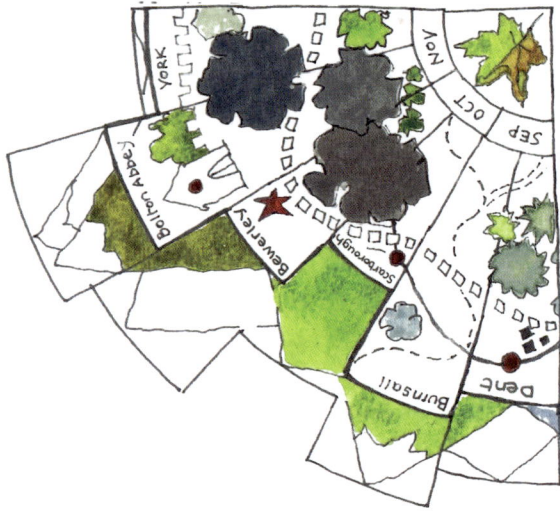

20

Bewerley

Distance 8 k / 5 miles
Time 2 to 3 hrs
Ascent 237 m

Roadside parking near the village green
Bewerley
HG3 5HS

Another favourite family walk which we always 'nick named' our Little Lake District.

On offer is the delightful Fishpond Wood with its beautiful tranquil lake. Our path climbs quite a steep pull up to Crocodile Rock and Yorke's Folly.

Yorke's Folly was built by John Yorke as a ruin in 1799. There are lovely stories of his benevolence in paying the local poor to help with the build.

More woodlands await in autumn splendour with more hidden 'tarns'. If children are tired or the weather and time are against you a quick descent can be made from Yorke's Folly back to Bewerley.

However the complete walk has it all - even a little moorland march and a little navigating through the hillside wood.

Don't forget to come back in late May lovely walker when those rhododendrons are in full flower - and you could be in Grasmere!

i Useful info

https://thefollyflaneuse.com/yorkes-folly-or-the-stoops-pateley-bridge-north-yorkshire/

Ordnance Survey

Map of Nidderdale
Fountains Abbey, Ripon & Pateley Bridge
298 1:25 000

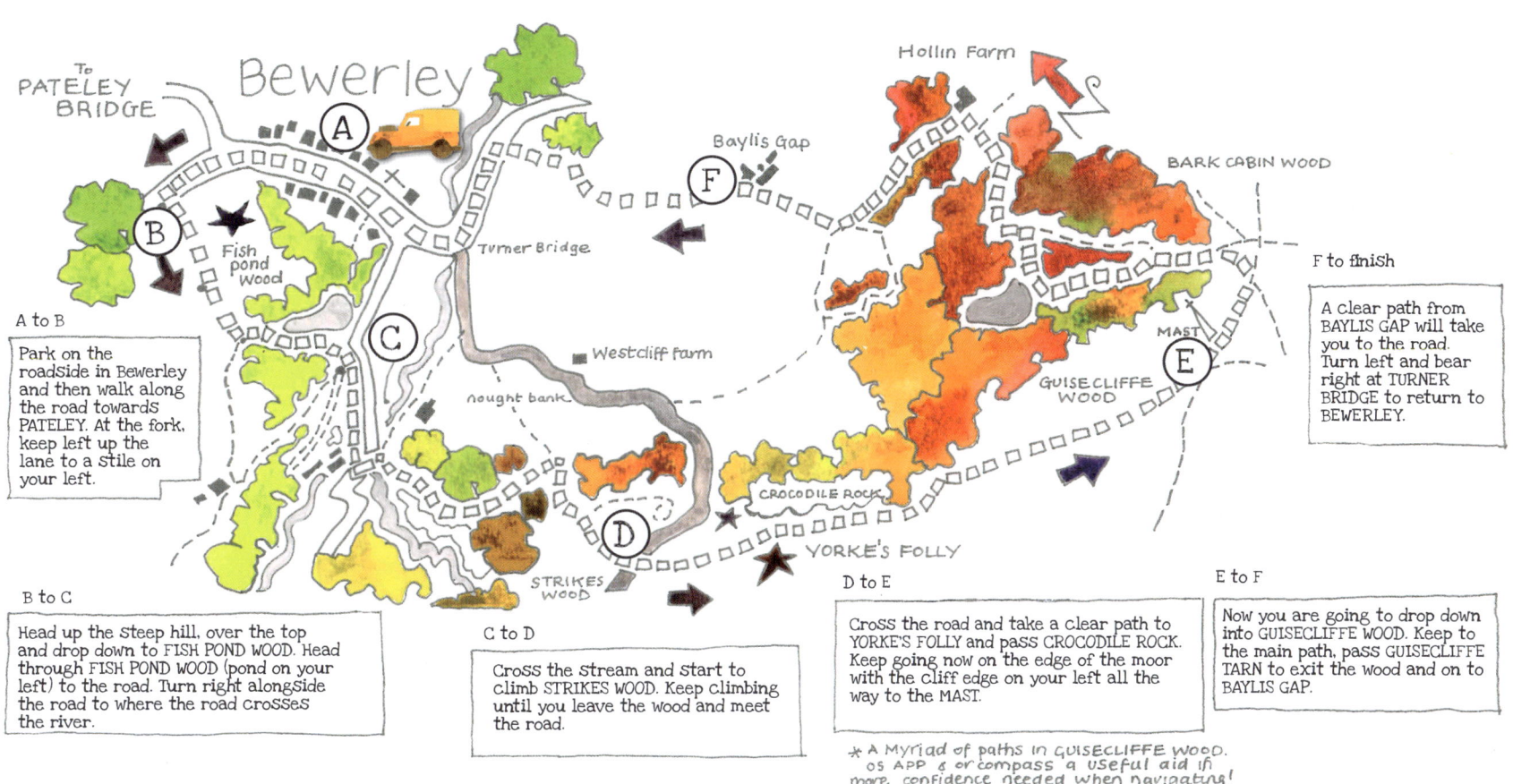

October

Our little Lake District

A lovely October walk in this mini lake district! Ponds, folly, woodlands all packed with seasonal colour. Easy to access with short cuts on offer, makes Bewerley a go-to family favourite.

A to B
Park on the roadside in Bewerley and then walk along the road towards PATELEY. At the fork, keep left up the lane to a stile on your left.

B to C
Head up the steep hill, over the top and drop down to FISH POND WOOD. Head through FISH POND WOOD (pond on your left) to the road. Turn right alongside the road to where the road crosses the river.

C to D
Cross the stream and start to climb STRIKES WOOD. Keep climbing until you leave the wood and meet the road.

D to E
Cross the road and take a clear path to YORKE'S FOLLY and pass CROCODILE ROCK. Keep going now on the edge of the moor with the cliff edge on your left all the way to the MAST.

E to F
Now you are going to drop down into GUISECLIFFE WOOD. Keep to the main path, pass GUISECLIFFE TARN to exit the wood and on to BAYLIS GAP.

F to finish
A clear path from BAYLIS GAP will take you to the road. Turn left and bear right at TURNER BRIDGE to return to BEWERLEY.

* A myriad of paths in GUISECLIFFE WOOD. OS APP & or compass a useful aid if more confidence needed when navigating!

● Autumn Splendour at Bolton Abbey - Bolton Abbey

● Firecracker City Walk - York

With much shorter days upon us a classic autumn walk around the environs of Bolton Abbey is a must. Easy to follow, Mother Nature in all her golden finery and a warming coffee to finish. A lovely place to catch up with friends (and their dogs!), the Cavendish Pavilion is our go-to 'let's meet up for a walk' destination.

November is also a great time to complete a 'proper' city walk. Our Firecracker Walk around the riverside and medieval majesty of York takes us around one of Europe's best loved cities. *A Walk around the Snickleways of York* by Mark W. Jones plots a path around the ancient snickets and ginnels of the city (very much worth adding to your library). We have included a couple of those hidden paths in our Firecracker Walk to give you just a taste!

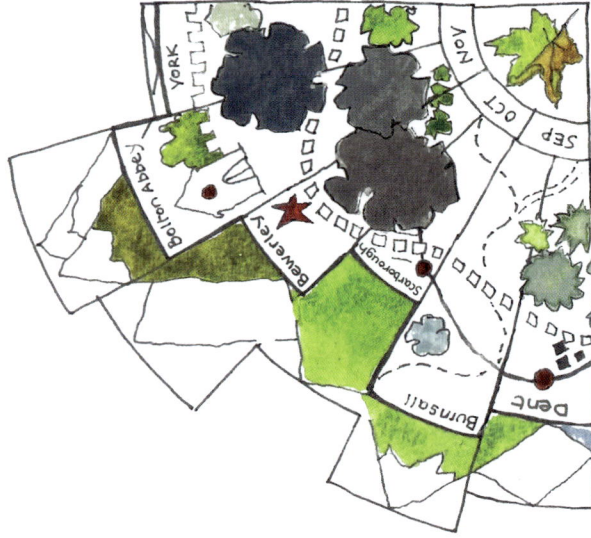

21

Bolton Abbey

Distance 13 k / 8 miles
Allow 4 hrs
Ascent 347 m

Park / start of walk
Cavendish Pavilion
Bolton Abbey Estate
BD23 6AN

 lovely walk from the Cavendish Pavilion at Bolton Abbey.

Parking at the Cavendish Pavilion (easy parking, café, loos and gift shop) our path heads south towards the Abbey to leave the crowds for a hilltop ramble before dropping back into the glorious Strid wood.

If time and or the elements are against you, a simple 5 mile / 8 k walk can be had by following the river north to Barden Bridge and back again south... following the river all the way. (See walk 8).

The Wood offers autumnal colours and diversity - clear paths all the way.

There are lots of little benches and stopping points around the wood.

Your return leg will be easy to navigate and not over busy if you avoid sunny Sundays.

The Bolton Abbey facilities and environs are a credit to the Devonshire estate.

Do check out their special events and trails for children.

i Useful info

To note - it's free to park at the Cavendish if you are a member.
£15 per car for non members.
More info https://boltonabbey.com

Your best map

Map of Yorkshire Dales - Southern & Western Areas
Whernside, Ingleborough & Pen-y-ghent
OL2 1:25 000
Nidderdale
298 1:25 000

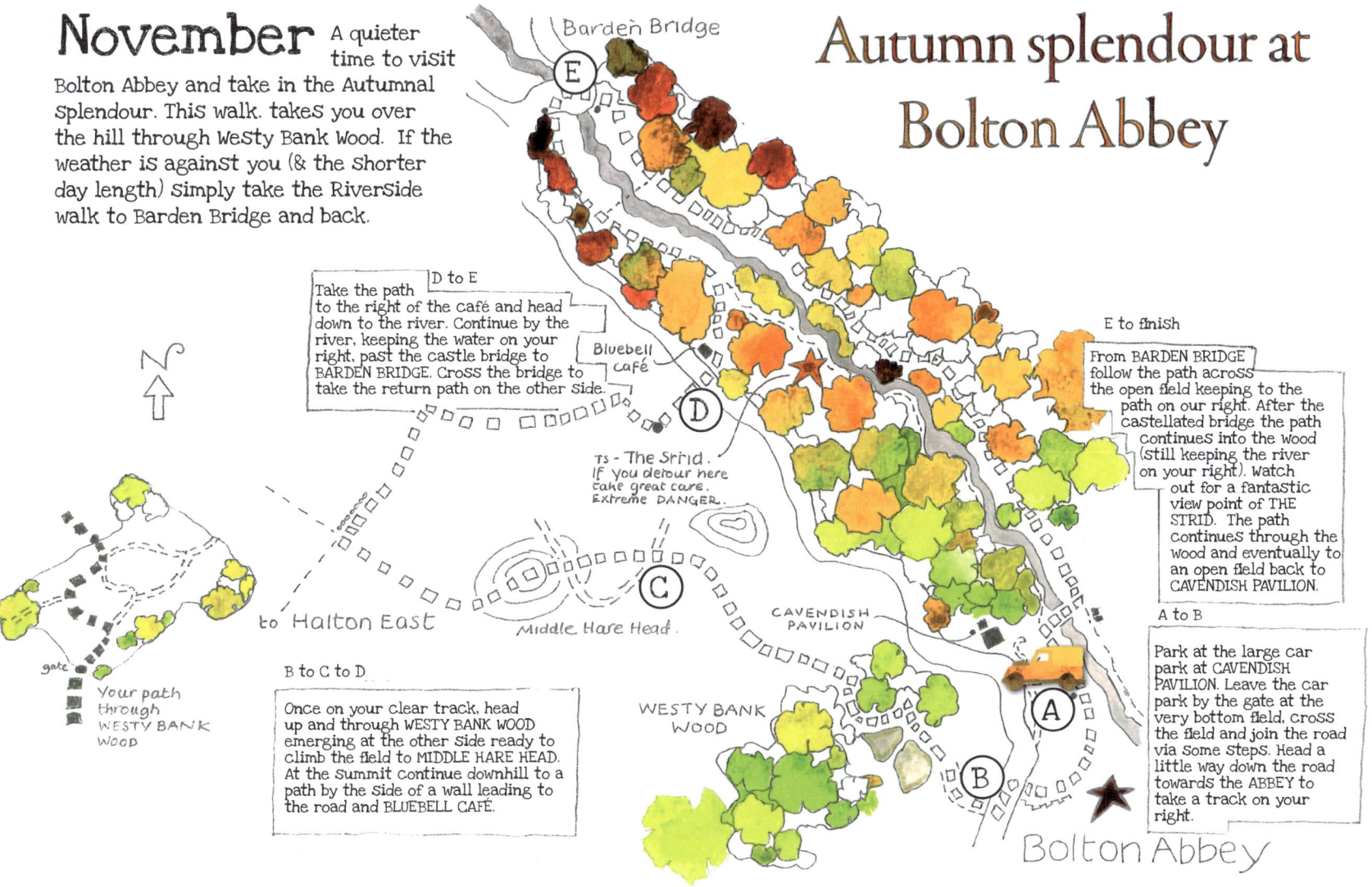

November is the perfect month to try our favourite city walk. If you are a regular visitor to the city, a local or first timer - November has the added attraction of the St. Nicholas Christmas market - something else for you to navigate!

If you are truly new to York ...we can only say ...stay a while. A most beautiful medieval city that is easily explored on foot ...with some of the finest history and architecture in the world.

Our walk (even though we are local) is one we never tire of. It constantly reminds us how lucky we are to have this amazing city on our doorstep.

Our walk takes us on two riverside strolls...

...a few snickleways, a cut through York's finest dept store and on the best urban footpath of all ... the bar walls.

Of course you could also time your walk to November the 5th and brush up on your treasonable history! You will pass St .Peter's School where Guy Fawkes was an 'old boy' and take refreshment in his birthplace - the Guy Fawkes Inn & hotel on Petergate.

There are lots of car parks and you can park and ride into York.

The new long-stay railway station (and national railway museum) car park has plenty of roomy spaces with the facilties of the station all to hand - and so we will start our walk here.

22

York

Distance 10 k / 6 miles
Time 3 hrs (if you don't stop!)
Flat

Start and Park
York railway station and
National Railway Museum Car park
24-44 Leeman Road
York
YO26 4XJ

i Useful info

No map needed but the excellent book and map
A Walk around the Snickleways of York by
Mark W Jones is one of our favourite extra guides to York.

Last little note is ...
York can flood very easily. Your riverside paths may disappear.
A walk all the way around the walls (approx 5 k) could be your fall back option, a day of 'Snickling' or simply ...explore!

Firecracker City walk

November is the perfect month to try our favourite city walk. If you are a regular visitor the city, a local or first timer, November has the added attraction of the St. Nicholas Christmas market - something else for you to navigate! Not to miss is the world class walk on the medieval walls and all those Snickleways.

E to F

Navigate across the city from MONK BAR to OUSE BRIDGE - our suggestion in the insert.

A to B

From the car park enter the railway station and leave on the other side via the short stay car park. A ramp and path takes you down to the river. Turn left and follow the river to CLIFTON BRIDGE.

B to C to D to E

Turn right over the bridge and right again to follow the river to the museum gardens. Cut across the garden to join the bar walls at BOOTHAM BAR ('C'). Follow the walls (by walking on them!) to ('D') and on to MONK BAR ('E').

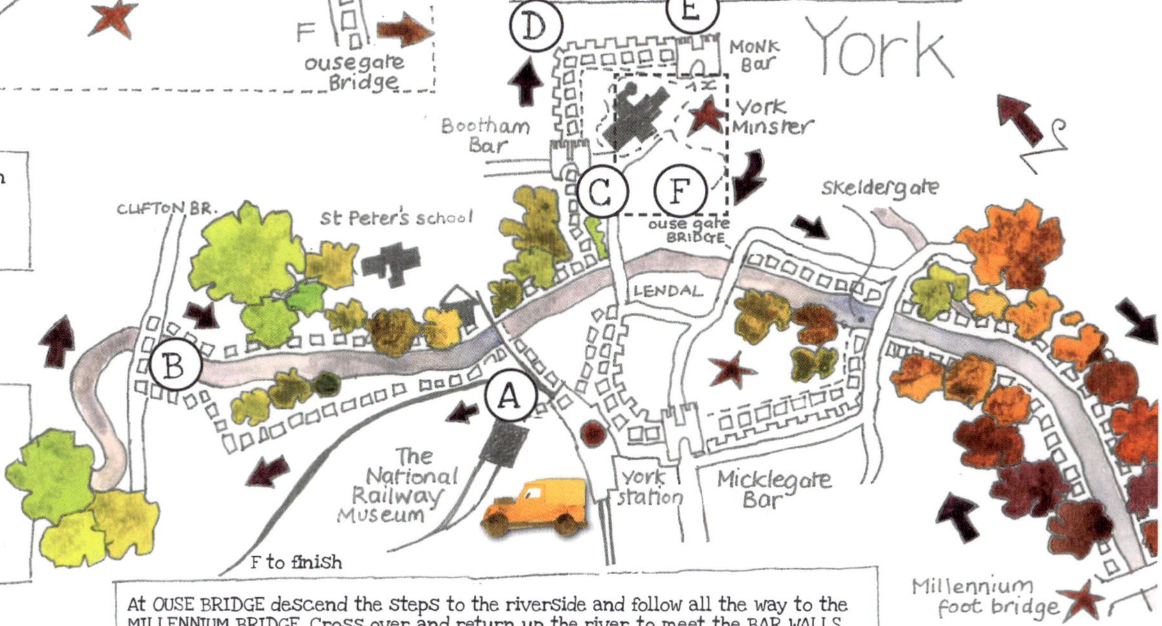

F to finish

At OUSE BRIDGE descend the steps to the riverside and follow all the way to the MILLENNIUM BRIDGE. Cross over and return up the river to meet the BAR WALLS at SKELDERGATE. Walk on the walls to YORK STATION to finish.

- 🟡 Yorkshire Stonehenge - High Knowle
- 🔴 The Mince Pie Special - Oxenhope, Haworth & Oakworth

The most enthusiastic walkers amongst us may find it difficult to keep our walking miles up during December with so many other distractions, but, the winter solstice will be upon us and once again a chance to ground our thoughts and ponder the wonder of the world around us.

Come Twixmas (that strange time between Christmas and New Year when we don't know what day it is!) a go-to walk is great to get the family off the couch or to meet up with friends.

Blowing away some cobwebs and walking off that Christmas pud is a must. And so, our final walk takes us to the Mince Pie Special at the Keighley & Worth Valley Railway. We can walk the footpath from Oxenhope to Keighley if we wish! Or, if tiny legs are with us, just Oxenhope to Haworth could be all that's needed.

Steam train at Oxenhope

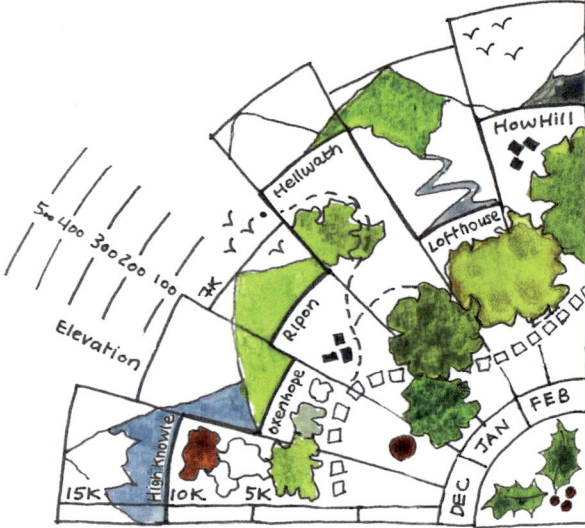

23

High Knowle

Distance 7.5 k / 4¾ miles
Time 2 to 3 hrs
Ascent 200 m

Park and start
Walkers' car park at
High Knowle
Swinton Bivouac Campsite
HG4 4JZ

★ star sights ★

the Druid's temple
long views to the North York Moors

Your best map
Map of Yorkshire Dales - Southern & Western Areas
Whernside, Ingleborough & Pen-y-ghent
OL2 1:25 000
Nidderdale
298 1:25 000

A lovely easy to follow path which takes in a section of the Ripon Rowel long-distance footpath with a riverside ramble to finish.

Our walk starts at High Knowle Bivouac campsite car park. There is a super café here, loos and little children's play park (part of the café). From here the Druid's Temple is our first call... but sadly not built by the Druids!

Our temple is a nineteenth-century folly styled on prehistoric monuments such as Stonehenge.

The Druid's Temple was built to alleviate local unemployment, allowing William Danby, a wealthy landowner of the time, to pay workers a shilling a day for their labour.

The site is maintained and cared for as part of the Swinton Estate.

Also to look out for are the stunning views to the North York Moors. Roseberry Topping and the White Horse can be seen from the first few fields of the walk - Quite a view!

All in all a lovely winter's day stroll in a stunning hidden corner of North Yorkshire.

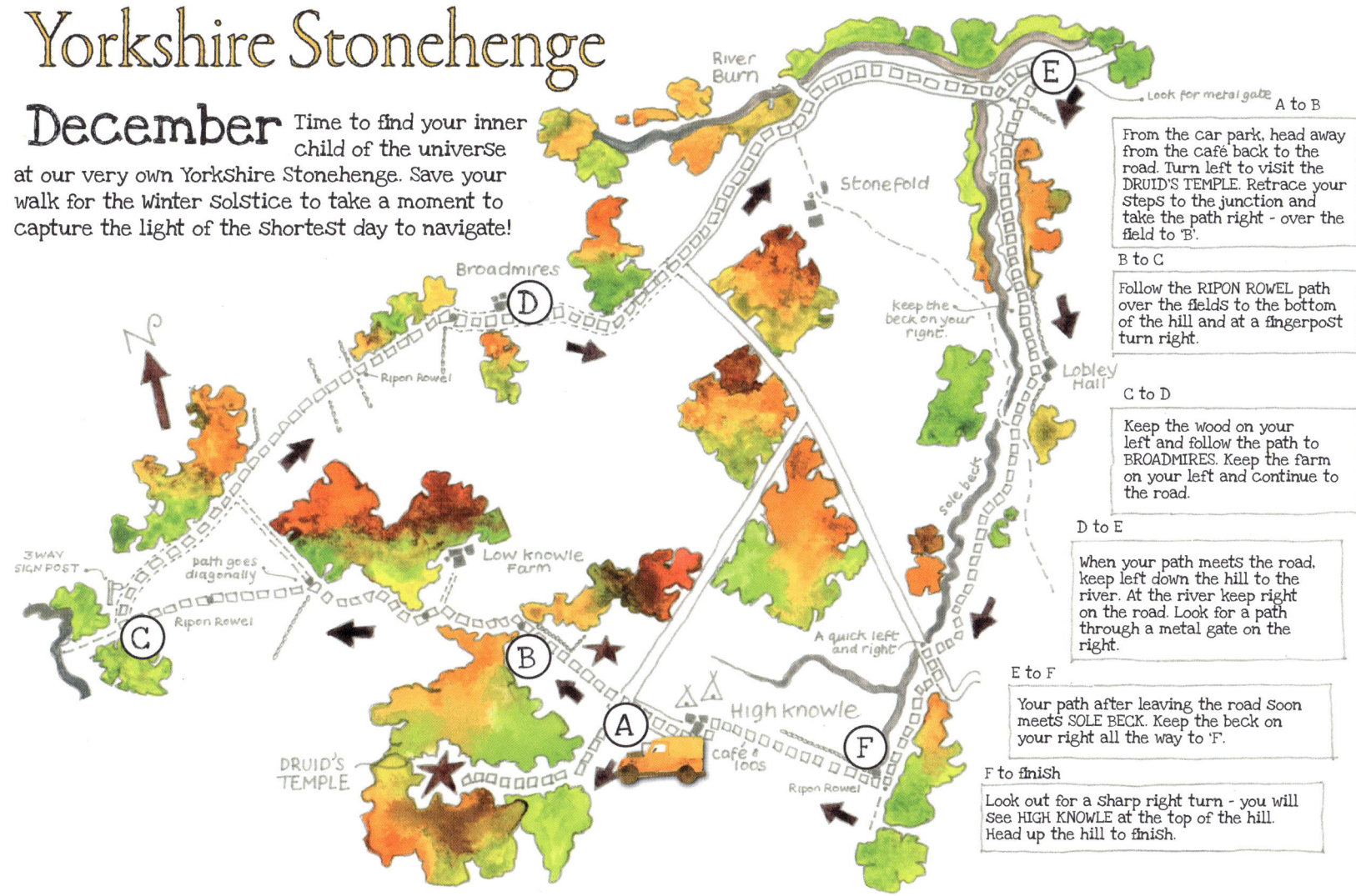

Oxenhope, Haworth & Oakworth

Distance 5 k / 3 miles (linear walk)
Time allow 2 to 3 hrs (1 hr walk plus train ride and exploring)
Ascent 139m

Park at
Oxenhope station car park
Mill Lane
BD22 9LB

Our little family walk is a fantastic way to get out and about over the Christmas to New year period. Our walk takes us back to Oxenhope and Oakworth (all of railway children fame) and never strays far from the Worth Valley line.

There are ample chances to experience the passing steam locos, wave (you will get 100s of waves in return!) and ride the return journey. The stations and locomotives are a credit to the volunteers who run the fantastic heritage Keighley & Worth Valley Railway.

A chance to step back in time, warm yourself by some real fires and ride the steam train with a mince pie and a pint if you fancy!

There are cafés, pubs and shops along the way.

Facilities are at all the stations with a café and shop at Haworth and Oxenhope.

Early bird bookings can be taken for the Elf express for the children in the run up to Christmas and of course the Mince pie specials from Christmas to New year!

And so lovely walker you have probably guessed we love our steam (another legacy from my steam 'buff' late father)

And ...as he was the one who suggested walking all those years ago and ...this railway ramble, his favourite walk ...our wave at the loco is always just for him.

i   Useful info

For more info and train times

https://kwvr.co.uk

Your best OS map

Map of South Pennines
Burnley, Hebden Bridge, Keighley & Todmorden
OL21 1:25 000

A little note
Heavy rain can cause flooding under the railway bridges... If so, simply head up the hill to the road and walk into Haworth via Ivy lane.

The mince pie special

December
Another chance to visit the famous Keighley & Worth Valley Railway - this time between Christmas and New Year to catch the Mince pie special. A simple linear walk with the promise of the return ride on the steam loco. A great family meet-up thing to do. A family tradition for us! We will see you there!

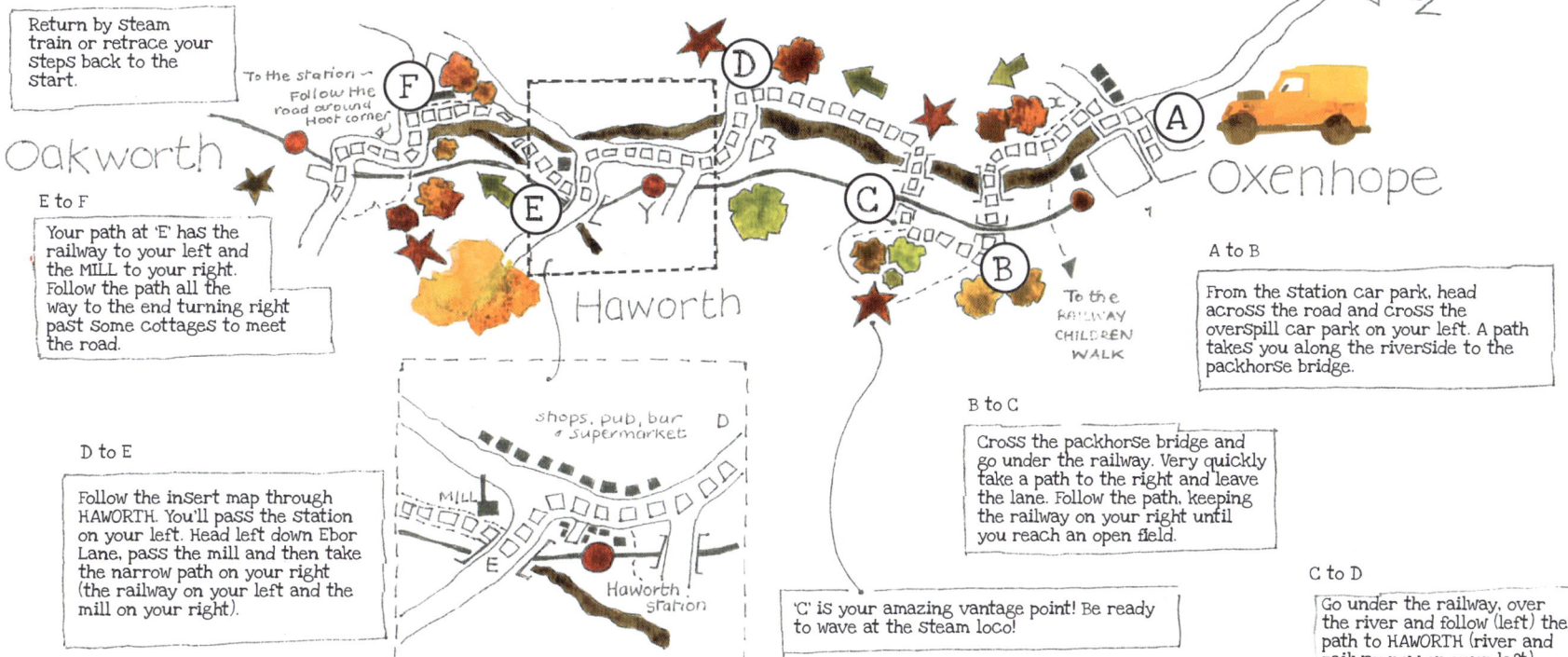

F to finish
Return by steam train or retrace your steps back to the start.

E to F
Your path at 'E' has the railway to your left and the MILL to your right. Follow the path all the way to the end turning right past some cottages to meet the road.

D to E
Follow the insert map through HAWORTH. You'll pass the station on your left. Head left down Ebor Lane, pass the mill and then take the narrow path on your right (the railway on your left and the mill on your right).

A to B
From the station car park, head across the road and cross the overspill car park on your left. A path takes you along the riverside to the packhorse bridge.

B to C
Cross the packhorse bridge and go under the railway. Very quickly take a path to the right and leave the lane. Follow the path, keeping the railway on your right until you reach an open field.

'C' is your amazing vantage point! Be ready to wave at the steam loco!

C to D
Go under the railway, over the river and follow (left) the path to HAWORTH (river and railway now on your left).

walking notes

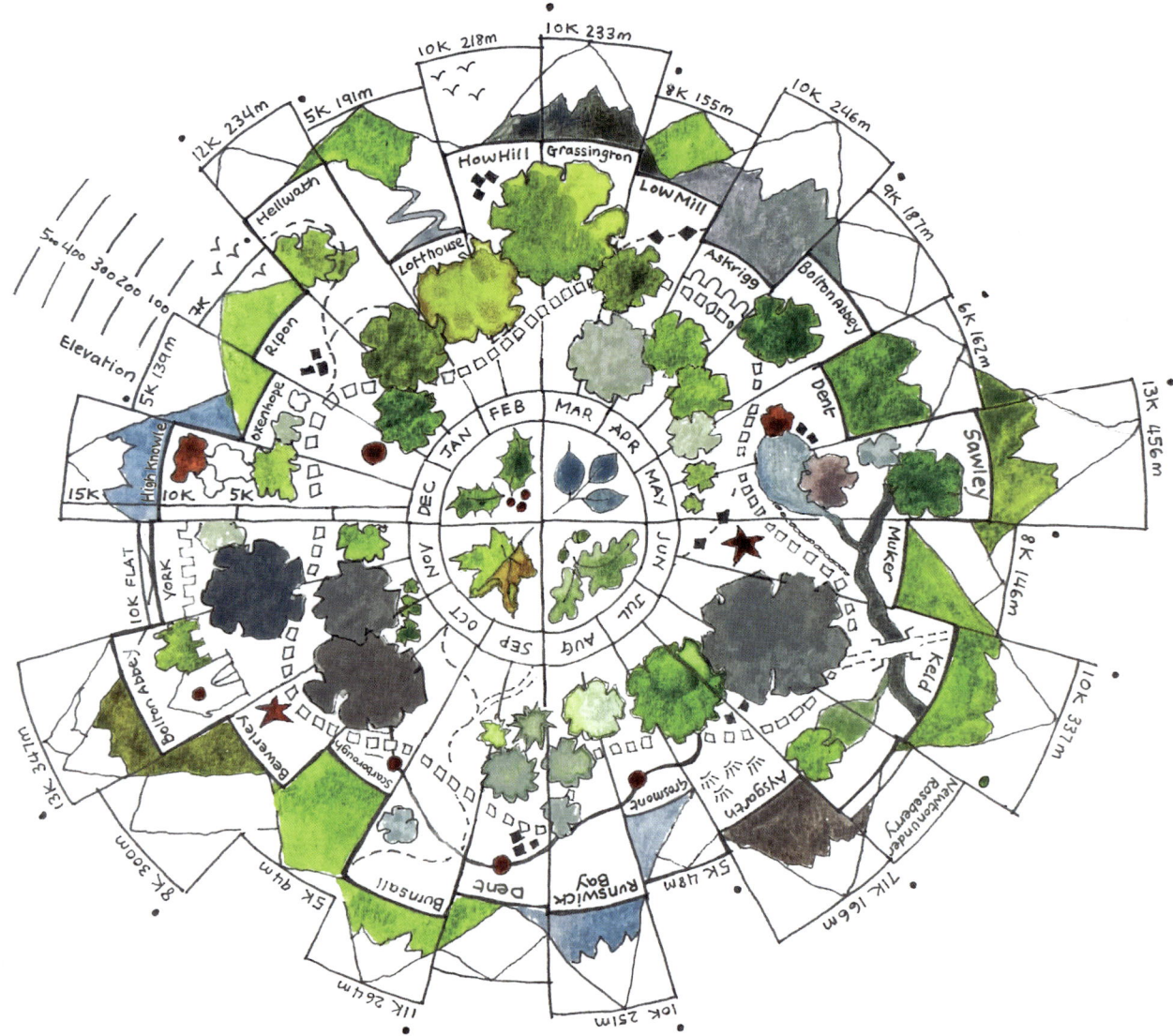